CU00663827

RUGBY
THE AFTERLIFE

RUGBY
THE AFTERLIFE
FORMER ALL BLACKS TELL THEIR STORIES

Wynne Gray

mower

A catalogue record for this book is available from the National Library of New Zealand

ISBN 978-1-988516-05-9

An Upstart Press Book
Published in 2018 by Upstart Press Ltd
Level 4, 15 Huron St, Takapuna 0622
Auckland, New Zealand

Text © Wynne Gray 2018
The moral rights of the author have been asserted.
Design and format © Upstart Press Ltd 2018

All rights reserved. No part of this publication may be reproduced or transmitted in any form or by any means, electronic or mechanical, including photocopying, recording, or any information storage and retrieval system, without permission in writing from the publisher.

Designed by www.cvdgraphics.nz
Printed by Everbest Printing Co. Ltd., China
Cover image: Getty

CONTENTS

ABOUT THE WRITER

Wynne Gray began his journalism career on the *Auckland Star* and the *8 O'Clock* before heading to travel and work in Europe and Australia. When he returned he became the senior rugby writer for the *New Zealand Herald* and attended more than 250 All Blacks tests and internationals around the globe, filing for the company newspapers and also online. He has written several books, been a guest panelist on Sky television, won a number of awards and is a life member of the New Zealand Sports Journalists Association.

INTRODUCTION

When the final whistle sounds and the payments cease, what plans do All Blacks have for their future?

How are they placed to deal with life outside the training fields, gyms, hotels and whiteboard sessions that have become their routine existence? What occupation do they turn to and what plans have they made for life after a professional rugby career?

Way back when, there was a clear definition between work and rugby. Great names in the game spent their time working in an office, at a trade or out on the farm mixed in with training then playing at the weekends. That distinction between work and play became blurred through the 1980s and 90s until, in the wake of Jonah Lomu's stunning exploits at the 1995 World Cup and pressure from media barons, the International Rugby Board declared rugby professional.

Some players just missed that pay dirt, others straddled the crossover years, while the rest have never known any different and filled in 'full-time sportsman' on their tax returns as rugby picked its way through two decades of professionalism.

For all of them, there was a finishing line, a final test appearance. Some made that choice; others had it made for them. Some All Blacks planned for life after rugby; others were more laissez-faire about the next chapter of their lives.

How did they handle that transition? Did they wait for guidance, have a lightbulb moment, take on some serious study or retraining or did they have the security of going back into a family business? How did a life in rugby protect or prepare them for experiences after the game, and how and why did they make the choices they did?

Rugby — the Afterlife explores how 23 All Blacks coped with that transition and came out the other side. They represent a range of players, some legends of the game, some who racked up fewer tests, but all provide a candid portrait of life after rugby.

MARK ALLEN

'Bull' Allen represented New Zealand in 27 matches as prop between 1993 and 1997, including in eight tests, and scored one test try. He led the Hurricanes in the Super 12 in 1996 and played 110 games for Taranaki. He was also captain of the short-lived Central Vikings in 1997.

The end came in a scrum against the Brumbies in '98 in a match I probably should never have started. My back was buggered.

I'd been fortunate to play in both the amateur and professional eras at my peak, and it looked like I was going to be a regular in the test team. Everything was lining up, but my marriage was just about stuffed because I was never home. Rugby took me away all the time and in those early days of professional rugby as captain of the Hurricanes, even if I wasn't playing I was promoting the team. I enjoyed a good public profile but was letting myself down on the home front.

People were asking why I got so much publicity when I wasn't even a regular test player. Laurie Mains preferred to pick Richard Loe because he was seen as a tighter player than me, while I preferred to run with the ball. It was a very interesting time. I had a good crack and was a reserve in about 30 tests. I played in 27 All Blacks games and eight tests, although I only started in one of those tests.

When I finished, I felt like I could have played a lot more games for the All Blacks and I felt I had failed. Blessed with success, but cursed with ambition.

I felt like I never quite achieved what I could have. I thought I could play more tests, but the question mark was always around my scrummaging. I was very visible doing other things around the field, but there was a perception I couldn't scrum. I had a few challenges as I had started as a prop late in my rugby career at 19, although I felt by the time I finished I had sorted it out. It's all about timing. Someone like Duane Monkley springs to mind; he could have been a wonderful All Black, but he didn't get the nod in his era.

At the time, the All Blacks had captain Sean Fitzpatrick, Craig Dowd and Olo Brown as a collective and they were the best front row in the world. It was as simple as that and it didn't make sense to break them up. I remember playing in the trials and getting to go alongside Fitzy and he was such a terrific scrummager.

There I was with my life at a crossroads with three young kids at that stage, a wife who'd had enough, and a decision had to be made. I thought if I continue playing — my back was giving me grief — did I want to be crippled by the time I got to 50?

I've reached that age now and feel I'm in great nick. I've looked after myself — so looking back, I made the right decision. I could have played a few more years if everything had hung together and played more tests, but at what expense? I have no regrets. I have five great kids and three grandkids, and a strong marriage. We're all still together and doing well.

I'd trained as an auto electrician and loved working for my father in Taranaki, but there wasn't really room in the business for me as well, so after rugby I started doing a lot of promotional stuff for companies, some commentating, TV work and presenting. We were living just out of Stratford and my wife Geralyn pointed out that while I'd given up rugby, I was still away doing promotional work, usually in Auckland and Wellington, and if that was going to continue, we needed to move.

Originally, we were going to shift into New Plymouth but decided if we were going to make a change we should go somewhere different, so we moved to the Bay of Plenty, to Omokoroa on the edge of Tauranga where Geralyn's parents had a property. I was picking up sufficient small jobs to keep paying the bills, not enough to ever get rich, but I was happy to spend more time with the kids and think about some ideas.

I had a bit of money from professional rugby and Geralyn had studied for a law degree, then went back to run the family sheep and beef farm when her father got sick. She was keen to continue farming, but that wasn't me, so we went into kiwifruit.

We lost heaps of money. We made a couple of bum calls and lost about a million bucks. At the same time, we were building a house in Bethlehem in Tauranga that was going to cost us $400,000 so I needed an income. The one good investment we had was in Omokoroa with Geralyn's family.

We had put money in to help her parents build a house, and so they put us up when we needed them.

At one stage during the global financial crisis of 2007/2008, I was working in four different jobs — with night shifts and long hours, travelling to Auckland, and also sat my real estate licence, but I'm not a great man for answering phones at night. I worked for a travel company and then a media company in Auckland.

Geralyn finished her degree and worked part-time, so we could keep our kids at Bethlehem College. Education is important to us. We both have a strong faith, and when we were struggling, our faith and church family helped us get through it. My parents helped us keep our kids in the school they were used to, by paying fees, and my in-laws were great too with their support, so we were very fortunate.

It was hard to ask for help and your pride gets a hit and you feel a bit of a failure after being reasonably successful. Now I know I can speak to my kids about what life is like on both sides of the fence, and they see me getting up early, going out the door to exercise or to work every day and that's a strong message about attitude and work ethic. Things like financial turmoil can blow you apart, but it drew us together and made us realise how lucky we were to have each other and our health. We all need to believe in something and our family has a strong faith in God. We got advice for our investment plans, but they still didn't work out. Although there were a few tough years, Geralyn and I worked through it.

One day I was watching Luke, my oldest son, play rugby and I don't know what it was, the Holy Spirit or a voice or whatever, but the thing that came to me was — would you be any happier now if you had all that other stuff? The simple answer was no.

I realised I had been chasing things thinking that would make me more successful, but I had been chasing the wrong things. You don't know you are doing it, but you are. I had a healthy marriage, healthy kids, I was still employable and fortunate I had a work ethic — and all that was worth a fortune.

At one point, I was working at night for a mate's building company. I'd done promotions with Christian Cullen in a supermarket and there I was, in a hi-vis jacket and helmet putting up shelving in the same place . . . and no one cared. Mahe Drysdale came along and looked at me and said, 'Is that you, Bull?' He jokingly said, 'Things must be tough, Bull,' and I said, 'Mahe, it's kind of you to stop and talk to me because lots of others don't bother.' He replied, 'Bull, I'll talk to you, but I'll have to send you an invoice.' What a down-to-earth, good guy.

Fortunately, I got asked by one of my son's friends to speak at a function for Genera Ltd, the biggest biosecurity company in Australasia, and that led to a job. They're a company which uses heavy-hitting fumigation for import and export goods such as logs and containers. Head office is at Mount Maunganui and they were rebranding the pest-management division as Genus. I was looking for something local and started as business development manager. There were five of us on staff then and the business has grown and now has 30-odd staff including subcontractors — and these days I manage the business. Rugby opened that door for me and I was able to walk right through that opening.

After years of promotional work, I was glad to have a steady income. I didn't have a Bull Allen business plan for my promotional company, but we did okay. I could have pushed it more, but I wanted to be a better father and husband and be with my family. That's what motivates me, that's my mantra now, and I didn't want to keep trading on being 'Bull Allen' the rugby player.

Being a good dad is worth striving for and you get great feedback. My older daughter Sarah is 29 and has three little ones so, yes, I am Grandad Bull. Geralyn and I have four kids: Luke is 22, Thomas is 20, Molly is 15 and my youngest fella James is 12.

Geralyn teaches English and literacy at Te Wharekura o Mauao, which is a Te Reo immersion wharekura in Bethlehem where the kids are amazing: bilingual, real team players and great at rugby too. By the end of the week Geralyn is exhausted, but she loves the work and feels if we can all make a bit of a difference that's the reward.

Life's good. We run a big bus, with four kids still at home and my mother-in-law living with us too. I'm coaching footy teams. I've coached the older boys who are 17 months apart and both played for the under-18 Bay of Plenty team the same season. I've coached Tai Mitchell, which is a rep team in the Bay that my youngest fella is in, and now he's in the Roller Mills Bay of Plenty Primary School team. He's a hooker and he goes well.

I haven't had a drink for years. It had to stop. I remember coming back from one rugby trip when I missed a flight and Geralyn picked me up and said, 'If you expect me to keep making excuses for you to your kids, I'm not going to any more. How is it you give your best to others and can't give us the same attention?'

It was simple; it had to stop. Life's been better since then. I love playing tennis, which I've picked up again after playing as a youngster, and a mate of mine has a ping-pong table and we get into great matches there. I swim and I'm into working with kettlebells and then into the sauna to stretch and recover. I'm enjoying every day as it comes. Why worry about tomorrow when the worries about today are enough? I want to enjoy life and see what unfolds.

FRANK BUNCE

Frank Bunce began his All Blacks test career in 1992 at second five-eighth, but thereafter was the linchpin at centre until 1997, in a legendary pairing with Walter Little (see later in this book). He ran up 96 test points, including 20 tries. Before his All Blacks debut, he represented Samoa in the 1991 World Cup. He played for the Chiefs in Super Rugby 1996–98, and for Auckland and North Harbour at provincial level. He also played for Castres club in France and Bristol in England.

About five years ago I got my first real job when I bought a tyre business in Thames.

Working for Sky and doing other rugby stuff was becoming a bit repetitive and one day my mate rang and asked me to go and help out at the opening of his shop in Thames. I wasn't that keen; I'd worked in a tyre shop when I was on school holidays and didn't fancy doing that again. Or so I thought.

Anyway, I ended up tagging along with him. The basics

were still the same, but the hydraulics and options were better. My mate Rob had bought the business and asked me to work with him for a few months. It turned out to be good timing. While working there, we lived out in the country on 21 acres at Kawakawa Bay with fresh air, horses and few neighbours and work was an easy hour drive away.

Carla, the mother of my two youngest kids Victoria, nine, and Josh, seven, fancied the idea of me doing some regular work because I wasn't doing a lot otherwise. (Oldest boy Chance is 31, Samantha is 25 and Jordan is 22.) I was full-on working, getting my hands dirty. I didn't mind it, and the physical stuff is fine. After all, I ran the roads on the garbo truck for ages and that was probably my best job as it kept me fit for footy, it didn't last all day and was a good excuse to get up each day.

After a couple of months working at the tyre business, I'd grown to like it so much that I bought it. It goes well and I've got a manager there, which gives me freedom to do any speaking at rugby clubs, chatting to schools and promotional stuff, and it puts money in the kitty. I look after myself and that's a better way to go.

Now I've moved to Cambridge, where Carla is originally from. We're set with horses on five acres of land and my kids are settled there and that means we will sell our place at Kawakawa.

Things have worked out okay. They could have been better, but my timing has usually been pretty good. I get invited to work at the sevens up in Hong Kong, Vegas and Chicago, and I have done some work for the consulate in Hawaii.

The good thing about rugby is you can make friends for life. If you, say, go to the States and find a rugby club and say where you are from, you have then got a new network of friends.

I go up to watch Manukau play club rugby a couple of times

a month, I watch All Blacks tests on television, attend the occasional reunion to catch up with some old mates or guys we rarely see, and I'll maybe watch a Friday game of Super Rugby, but there are way too many games on the calendar.

Going back a bit there was the charity event Fight for Life, and TV shows like *Dancing with the Stars*. Fight for Life was great, but not what I'd call fun. I fought in Australia once and then also up in England. I enjoyed the training and all the people, the sense of achievement and the after-match, but I didn't like the fights.

I fought in a London charity bout that Chris Cairns put on and got 20K for that. I fought former England player Chris Sheasby and knocked him out. I think I had more support than he did that night in what was my last fight. The training was getting harder and the fighting part was not enjoyable. Lance Revill was my trainer and he operated like Laurie Mains. I find I respond to that just as I did to Albie Pryor at Manukau. I'm a lazy bugger who has to be pushed.

It didn't seem right trying to punch someone in the head. In rugby you'd get one or two in then it was stopped, but boxing was round after round.

In *Dancing with the Stars*, I could have been a whole lot better if I'd trained more. The worst part was standing in the wings before you go on when the compere belts out a 'Welcome to the stage Frank and Krystal doing the samba.' They're all telling you to smile, but you go out there and work like a robot. With the cameras on you, you are not comfortable and you never feel like letting yourself go.

I agreed to doing those shows because when you retire you're not sure what skills you're going to need and you go and try these other things. You're competitive. All my life in rugby you train all week to play and win at the weekend, have a few beers and then start again. I'd been doing that all my life and then one day it's not there.

My last game for the All Blacks was at Twickenham in the 26-all draw with England at the end of 1997 and my previous test on that ground was also against England in 1993 when we lost. I'd opened my big mouth — and that was another lesson I learned — and said how we hate the English and there's no way we are going to lose, and we did. We didn't have a great team that year and it was an awful game.

In 1998 I was keen to play, but the problem was John Hart didn't know I had been overseas. In those days there was an off-season and clubs always rang asking if you could play for them.

He organised a few things around Kevin Roberts and Lions Breweries that kept me in the country, but it was always in my mind to head away and play. I wanted to have a look somewhere else and I wasn't really that interested in going to the UK; I wanted to go somewhere with a different culture, like France.

We used to speak every year with Harty about our ideas and it was at that point I said I wasn't going to make the 1999 World Cup — I was losing a bit of interest.

Physically, I could have made it, but mentally I could not be bothered with the training and the travelling, and it had got to that point, so I told him. He was good about it — he said, 'Okay, we'll manage the rest of your career until you figure out how you want to end it. You decide how you want to go out, starting games or coming off the bench or a mix, pick a date when that's it, I'll leave it up to you.'

So I had plans to play through the '98 season and then just phase out. Then an opportunity came up through Joe Stanley. 'Hey,' he said, 'I've got this French club who are interested, and they want you to go up and have a look.' That was shaping to be a bit difficult because we had the All Blacks trial coming up, but we had a week when there was a bye or a gap in Super Rugby and we thought we could make the travel work.

I think they gave Joe about 30K to take care of getting us up there and he asked me to go with him. So Joe and I, and Miriama Smith, who I was going out with at the time, went and had a look at Castres.

The visit would have worked except that the French pilots were on strike for more pay because of the Football World Cup. A couple of our flights were cancelled, which meant we were late getting our connections and that created problems.

It had sounded great, tripping around, but when we got to Paris our flight out was cancelled and the replacement we got via Germany arrived but we had missed the connection back to Singapore and Auckland. The next one we could get wasn't for two days.

We were holed up in a hotel room and Joe says, 'You've got to ring Harty and tell him you won't be back on time.' Both Joe and I had received messages from him so here's me thinking, 'Oh bugger it, I'll ring him. It'll be early morning in Auckland and his secretary will probably answer it and that'll break the ice because she'll go in and tell him it's me.'

Ring, ring. 'John Hart speaking.' That threw me straight away. 'Oh, Harty, it's Frank, Frank Bunce . . .' and then it started. I just held the phone out from my ear while he went for it for about 30 seconds — Joe could hear him across the room. He wasn't happy. He said he'd had to lie to people and didn't know what was going on — not being able to tell people where his players were and that wasn't good enough.

Then he said get home as quick as you can, and I'll see you

at the airport and we'll sort it out. We arrived in Auckland and Harty thought Joe was drunk, and that reinforced what he thought the pair of us were like together, but Joe had actually taken some sleeping pills, which had not completely worn off. The next day we turn up and Harty tells me he can't pick me because I've done this, that and this.

'You can't just show up and play in an All Blacks trial. I can't pick you; that's the way it is,' and that was pretty much my career.

I didn't worry too much then, but later I was disappointed in myself, and I'd go to a couple of the games and miss being part of it. I'd see guys playing and think I could be out there doing alright. I didn't handle it very well and that was my fault. When you know me, you can see how that can happen because to this day my organisation is not wonderful.

After Super Rugby finished I went to Castres. I was keen on playing over there, but what I found hard was that they do things so differently from how we do them, and that was my problem. I never realised all this until I thought about it later. You shouldn't go there and fight it; you have to go there and play along with it, accept that this is the way they do it and you add little pieces instead of asking all the time why we are training this way, why we are spending time on this. That was my issue — and then I injured my Achilles training on the morning of a game.

It was a team run, but not like the low-key captain's run we have; it was more like a full-blooded contact session. I had to do about three months' rehab, which was really boring, and it was a small town and you find out people talk in those places. Then I had a car accident while on the vino and that got more airplay.

I loved my time there and my advice now to people going over there would be not to say this is how we do it in New Zealand, just go with the local flow and accept what they do.

My playing career was winding down, but I'm not thinking about what I'm going to do after that. Not at all, because that's my nature and I don't plan ahead. When you're younger you don't think it's ever going to come to an end; you think it'll go on forever, even though I started my test career late. I played a few games for the Baabaas and then went to Bristol because Bob Dwyer coached the Baabaas and suggested I come on a short-term contract just before the 1999 World Cup.

Because of the Rugby World Cup, clubs were able to bring in players on short deals and I played there for two months. It was too good not to at about £5000 a game, cash. He said, 'Come up. I'll pay you per game and there'll be a house, a car and expenses.' I had a great time and was still not thinking about anything else.

I got involved in a little TV work there and then for TV3 following tours and did some work for TVNZ as well, which was enough to keep me afloat. You might follow a tour and be away for a month and add on some time to visit and there's two months and something else comes up like a weekly show on TV3.

I followed the All Blacks tour with them and ran into Mathew Vaea who was coaching Italy with Brad Johnstone and was also coaching a club team there. I'd known him from our 1991 Samoan side. I stayed with him and he asked me to help coach the club's backs. We met the club people and signed a contract.

I came home, sorted my stuff out and went back for three years. The lifestyle and semi-professional life at the Rovato club, halfway between Milan and Venice, right by some beautiful lakes, suited me and there were other Kiwis there as well. We were third division before we got promoted, but the standard was way below that of club rugby back home.

It meant I didn't have to think about what else I was going to do. All this chat and recall makes me think I'm lazy, but let's go with 'relaxed'. I could still run then and had to keep up but did not get into the middle of trainings. Eventually, I had enough of Italy and wanted to come home.

Before then they flew my three eldest kids up every year and they stayed for a while, which was great. Jordan played in junior tournaments and they all picked up the language. I was okay with Italian by the end; my reading and general conversation were fine. Rovato was the size of Taupiri, a very traditional town with one main street, and I had an upstairs apartment across the road from a really nice restaurant with a few nice coffee bars down the road.

Much of your time was spent in a short triangle. The restaurant owner would ring up Mat and me and say, 'We have a new dish tonight, do you want to come in?' 'Yep, we'll be along after training.' We'd get there about 9 pm and he's giving us some wine and food so long as we talk to him.

From Italy I'd go and do stuff for New Zealand television when the All Blacks were touring. I'd commute to Ireland for work, and there was time to have the kids up there and then I'd visit home.

On one trip back there was a chance meeting with new Auckland coach Pat Lam. He asked me what I was doing, and I told him I wasn't doing anything. He wanted a defensive coach; I said yes. That was it. I had no official training — all I knew was what I knew.

It was an eye-opener, as times had changed. You heard talk about guys not wanting to live in the past and they didn't need to hear about this, that and the other or want you to be too negative. Give them a hug instead of a kick up the arse. Carlos Spencer had gone from being the rookie to the old man and he was up on a pedestal like Gary Whetton was for us in the All Blacks.

It was different, but I don't think the changes had created improvement. It was all way too technical and everything was broken down into micro-pieces, and you could see players struggling with that. Trainings were complicated.

Any team I coach, like Manukau Rovers, I ask: 'Can you catch, run and pass? If you can't I'll help you, and this is the ball — use it.' I coached Melani Nanai at Manukau and we had some good backs. They would ask me what they should do in situations and I'd say, 'I don't know, use your eyes and instincts. You guys figure it out. Try this and that, but it's up to you, depends what the opposition are doing, so play what's in front of you.'

Rugby has got way too technical in the backs. Forwards need technical help, but in the backs you are there to run fast, tackle hard, use your flair, draw and pass and think. I'll ask them about their defensive patterns, their attack moves, their tactics and that's done.

Then I'll look over at the forwards who are still battling away.

Shorter and sharper the better, I think. Backs are different and they don't need long-winded ideas. Training is about skills, agility and being aware of space.

In 2005 I was technical advisor for Samoa, but I didn't do much. I never really wanted to be a coach and still don't and can't think of anything worse than being a full-time professional rugby coach. I'm happy to help, give advice, go and help, especially with young fellas because you can spot talent.

I'm president of Manukau now and coached them for about four years with my brother-in-law Tony Barchard who played for Samoa and Counties. Our main work was on fitness. Hayden Roe is our coach; I helped him for three years when he coached Thames Valley in Heartland rugby. We got them organised to a certain point and then told them to let rip.

ADRIAN CASHMORE

Adrian Cashmore played two tests, in 1996 and 1997. As a goal-kicking fullback and occasional winger, he played Super Rugby for the Blues 1996–2000 and the Chiefs 2004–2005, and for Bay of Plenty and Auckland at provincial level. He also played for Toyota in Japan and for Welsh team the Ospreys in the Celtic League.

My brief All Blacks career coincided with that really overrated guy, Christian Cullen — that's what I tell everyone! I played two games on the wing in my life and they were both test matches. I didn't know what the hell I was doing, but I was happy to play for my country.

Then I played in Japan, came back and was doing my papers and selling real estate for the old man in the Bay of Plenty and I was going to retire from rugby. But my name was down on a standby list for any Super Rugby side and I got a call to go and help the Chiefs.

I didn't think too much of office work so had two more years with the Bay and then got a random call from Ospreys asking me to play for them. I initially wasn't keen, but they kept ringing me and as I had nothing to lose and had never used an agent, I put my asking price up a bit, asked for a few things and told them my back wouldn't let me goal-kick. After seven games with them, I messed up my back again and came home. It was pretty major, so it was all over then.

That's when I had to have a serious think about what I was going to do. I always knew I was coming back to New Zealand, and there was a safety valve for work with the real estate. Wales asked me to stay and do some coaching, but that never appealed. I loved playing, and they were great years when you meet fantastic people and I had great times, but I wanted to get out and get home to a new path.

I jumped into the real estate business and thought I'd give it a really good crack.

I started selling commercial real estate and continued for about two and a half years. I really enjoyed the work but wasn't sure it was the right fit for me. However, it gave me job security and some income while I thought about what I wanted to do next. That was the key thing. I always say to the guys who are finishing up now that if they are thinking about coming home they have got to think about work.

It doesn't matter what it is; you need something to get up for each morning, something to go for. I have seen guys without that drive. There are a few real horror stories. That's life, I guess.

I walked into the old man's office one day and told him I liked real estate but it wasn't for me and basically left. He wasn't that happy about it.

About that time, Robin Brooke owned the New World supermarket out at Gate Pa. I saw a bit of him around Tauranga, so I went to see him and have a chat about the grocery business.

I think I got caught up in the image of the New World and Pak 'n Save high rollers and thought a bit of that work would be great. They did pretty well, so I thought I'd jump into it and went down the New World owner-operator path. I did some work for Robin, did some training and then jumped into a Four Square supermarket.

I was working behind the counter in Tauranga where people would walk in and ask, 'Are you that rugby player? Gee, what happened?' They were wondering why I was working as a checkout operator at a Four Square, but I was classed as an external and had to train in the Foodstuffs programme to make my way up the ladder to be able to buy a Four Square. I put in about four contract offers for Four Squares around the Bay of Plenty and there was even one in Murupara that I considered — it's a bloody good Four Square.

It never happened. I couldn't get a contract in place because the owners wanted far too much, so I put that idea aside and started looking at a whole lot of different businesses.

This is where I was lucky, through rugby and working, that I had a bit of cash to live on. I was doing odd jobs while I looked at all these business ideas and must have spent eight to 12 months looking for something. I talked with a business broker in Tauranga and a number of guys in Auckland looking at businesses for sale.

Richard Coventry was my go-to man. We played together up in Japan and he's an accountant, now in a massive job as chief executive of the Perry Group in Hamilton. He helped me look over business numbers and so on.

I have always worked on the theory that you have to surround yourself with people who know way more than you. It's a pretty simple philosophy, and I think the problem with a lot of guys is they are too afraid to put their hand up and ask questions and see people. Why wouldn't you? Nine out of 10 people will help you. You get a good lawyer and accountant and go from there.

I was looking at all sorts of businesses in 2010 when, out of the blue, a business broker in Tauranga rang and said he had a couple of guys who had started a meat-processing business and were looking for someone with some capital to come into the business.

We lined up a meeting, met the guys — one I knew through a mutual friend — and I liked them and what they were doing and walked out of the meeting to say to my people, 'I'm in.' It was that quick. I had been frustrated and I was getting desperate, so the timing was right.

You have a little money in reserve, but with a wife and three kids and money drifting through your fingers I was pretty keen to jump into something. Richard looked over the figures and my gut feeling was that this was right for me.

They had a small business in Birch Avenue, an industrial area in Tauranga, and it was a baptism of fire. I jumped in there and we had just picked up a contract to supply 400,000 lamb shanks into Australia and had less than a month to get it done.

Nick Neilson and Glenn Lange were my two business partners. Nick went to Aussie to run it and I started in the food-processing plant in Tauranga, but two days later got a call to get over to Oz to help for two or three days.

I flew over and was there for a month in south-western Sydney working 20-hour days and sleeping in the plant, but we got the job done. However, it pretty much broke Nick and we ended up buying him out. I was a wreck too and smelled like lamb for ages; I pitied the poor woman sitting next to me on the plane home.

I kept thinking of the bigger picture, though, and reckoned that one day I would be laughing about that start to the business. It was tough. We were a small operation supplying the North Island with a lot of marinated meats, beef, pork and corned silverside and hitting that lower end of the market with volume. Our largest competitor was Hellabys in Auckland, a massive multi-million-dollar business with extensive farms and infrastructure. We were just this little business in Tauranga. We took a bit of their market share, so they dropped their prices and that killed us. We thought we had to look elsewhere.

Long story short, we rang a guy in Dunedin who had a company called Fishers, which is who we are now. It is coming up 100 years old, but in 2009 it was put into receivership. I rang the landlord who bought the company from Fishers and suggested we fly down and talk to him about using the plant to help us service the South Island.

Glenn left school at 15 and got into butchery and was self-taught in terms of business. For 20 years he worked for Top Hat in Australia running their operations, then Seamart in Auckland, so he'd been in food operations for a long time.

We flew down and at the end of the meeting, Glenn asked if they would sell. The owners said no, but that evening I got a phone call saying they had reconsidered. We did the deal without telling our wives and when I got home Kylie asked me how it went. All I said was: 'Pretty good — and we might be moving to Dunedin.'

That was in November with the holidays approaching fast and with all sorts of financial issues to get sorted, but we got it all done by Christmas. Six weeks after agreeing to buy the business, I was living in Dunedin. Kylie was alright with that but was left to sell the house and arrange for all our belongings and our family to move down south. They all love it in Dunedin now and it is a massive opportunity.

I was right into work here in January 2012 and our three kids, Ollie, Milla and Zach, were all into their schools from the start of the first term. A mate of mine owned a house in Dunedin and worked on the oil rigs up in Singapore and the day we arrived, we went to stay at his place and I took him back to the airport and he flew out for a month.

We kicked the business off and had to do some research about housing and schools, but the beauty of being in footy was I knew a heck of a lot of guys down here. I was on the phone to John Leslie, Kees Meeuws and John Blaikie and they've all got great partners, friends and connections and were all very helpful.

It was a crazy time, but we had lived overseas because of rugby and this was just another move. It wasn't a major. Dunedin grows on you and you make the most of Central Otago and the likes of Arrowtown and the wider region — like last year when we flew into Dusky Sound in a chopper to go free diving for massive crayfish; it was out of this world.

We all have a piece of each other about Auckland against the Bay or Otago versus Waikato, but when the footy is on it's all of us in Dunedin against the visitors.

We inherited a staff, but at that stage we couldn't employ them all, although we kept most on and have since employed more. When we took over we had a turnover of just under $4 million with a staff of more than 30 and now we are doing $12–13 million with 25 staff. In Tauranga, the banks didn't really want to touch us, but they are all over us now.

Glenn operates the financial side of the business and I run the sales side with a tele-sales person, talking to butchers around

New Zealand. I spend plenty of time on the road travelling around the country about six times a year.

That's part of business and you get in and do it. I think back to my footy days and use those lessons to refine issues, keep things simple and work out solutions. There are plenty of lessons that transfer from sport to business, and I think that is crucial.

At times in sport and business you wonder what you are going to do and you are not always right, but you have to have a go.

When I was picked for Auckland, I was young but learned quickly from coach Graham Henry and the older, experienced players. The mentality of guys in that group taught me a lot about life in general and how to face challenges. It was a special team to be part of and I'm sure the training we did would be right up there with what the players of today do.

We are in a good position in our business, which operates five days a week. Unlike the Tauranga business, we have all the machinery needed here in Dunedin and the volume and systems are well organised and run by division managers. It has to be organised and Glenn knows that side of the business inside out.

We sell to domestic markets and have tried to build on the very solid foundation we have got at Fishers. After getting some expert IT help, we have launched a new meat-to-your-door online business that is pretty full-on. We are also conscious about the necessary family/work/play balance and we lead a special life down here.

We go fishing, diving, water-skiing or snow skiing on our weekends. I didn't want to go down the rugby coaching path; I'm prepared to help out and watch my kids play basketball, netball, soccer and gymnastics, but if we have time we take off.

As a family, you can't beat it.

I have done the 125-kilometre Hawea mountain-bike ride, which was a stunning event: tough but cool. I completed it in about six hours but want to do better next time as I've still got the competitive juices flowing.

It's like an old-style New Zealand living in Dunedin, with more freedom, rather than being financially geared up to the eyeballs. Dunedin has a heap of potential; it's a great region that is very proud and traditional. I'm not sure if we'll still be in the same business in a decade because we're always looking at other opportunities. But I'd love to still have it and build on it.

I've got another business with my brother in Tauranga that deals in liquid waste and is going very strongly. We dispose of waste from restaurants and boats and have a long-term consent in place to do so.

Glenn and I would love to create a commercial portfolio now so that in 10 or 15 years' time when I'm past the half-century mark, I hope I don't have to work — that's the plan anyway. We're in a good spot and I've been lucky. At one stage, I was given advice about not getting into a partnership, but I was not long out of the rugby team environment and that emphasises pulling together and I thought I could make it work.

Meeting Glenn, doing some due diligence, and having good legal and investment advice and a bit of luck have gone a long way. We drew up a shareholders' agreement, but we've never had to open that envelope, as it's been perfect.

MATTHEW COOPER

Matthew Cooper first played for the All Blacks in 1987, but he did not get his test start until five years later against Ireland, when he scored 23 points for a record on debut. He played from 1992 to 1994 and in 1996, including eight tests, chiefly as a goal-kicking second five-eighth, running up 55 points. He also represented Croatia and played Super Rugby for the Highlanders and the Chiefs, and turned out for Hawke's Bay and Waikato.

After finishing up with the All Blacks after a great tour of South Africa in 1996, I played a World Cup-qualifying test for Croatia two years later. I am a very proud Croatian through my mother's side of the family. My grandparents came out to New Zealand from what was Yugoslavia in the 1920s, and Mum always imparted that family history and it gave us a strong sense of who we are.

Back in the late 1990s, the Croatian team had a strong New Zealand connection as they tried to get to the 1999 World

Cup. Frano Botica had already played a few games for Croatia, and I got a call from Antony Sumich, now Father Sumich, who was involved with Auckland Marist, asking about my interest. Straight away I said I was keen but needed to know if that was possible.

My All Blacks days were effectively over. I was 32 and, at that time, you were able to play for another country anyway, but I wanted to check the implications for Super Rugby and Waikato and got New Zealand Rugby's assurance it wouldn't have an impact on my selection for those teams.

The idea of playing for Croatia struck a chord with me; it was about who I am and where I have come from and I talked it through with my family. Then I spoke to Frano and my former Hamilton Marist and midfield partner Andrew Matijasevich, while Tony remained very persistent.

The entire experience was amazing from my arrival in Zagreb then going down to Split and being welcomed strongly by the team. We were to play Italy on 6 June 1998 in a qualifying game at Makarska on Croatia's Dalmatian coast. Italy knew I was on my way and Frano had been there, so they picked a fairly strong line-up to play us. It was a competitive match, a close game at 39–27 to Italy, but before that, midway through the week Tony asked me if I'd like to go home, to see where my ancestors came from.

That was way up in the mountains in the little village of Prapatnice and a minibus was arranged for Tony and me to travel up there, but when we left the van was full of teammates who thought the three-hour trip would be quite special.

I knew about the larger town of Vigorac, which is at the top of the mountains about 10 minutes from Prapatnice where my grandfather was born. We saw the road sign and when we arrived at that town all the people popped their heads out the windows and the older women, all in their traditional black garments, fell to the ground in tears because Mum had corresponded with them and knew we were coming. It was a very emotional moment and one I'll never forget.

We stayed and had a feast and later in the afternoon they took me to a broken-down building where my grandfather was born. In 2008, my parents Pat and Tricia and my sister Ana and her family made the same emotional trip.

When we lined up later that week to play the test it felt right. There was real legitimacy about playing for Croatia rather than the situation where some players have used flags of convenience.

Once my rugby was done about 1999, my path in life was looking a little confused. It was the end of the millennium, I'd achieved many of my dreams in playing for the All Blacks, winning the Ranfurly Shield, playing Super Rugby and for Hawke's Bay then Waikato for so many years. I was married with a son and needed to find and establish a career.

I decided I wasn't going to play overseas. I might have pushed through a few more seasons, but there were risks about that with injury and diminished links back home, and I decided it was better to make use of my profile around the Waikato region.

For all those who go overseas, most don't get the leverage from their profile that the likes of Dan Carter, Charlie Faumuina or Aaron Cruden do. An awful lot of players, and I would be amongst those, do alright but usually still have to come back to New Zealand and earn a living.

I linked up again with Lion Nathan who had supported me in the early part of my career and worked for them as a sales representative. They were very helpful with the 'art' of business, the importance of the brand and the professional development they provided. They were competitive, liked to win and a lot of the ethos of working with Lion connected to sport.

However, it wasn't going to be a long-term career because of a fundamental clash of values about selling stacks of beer but knowing that at the end of each month I had to load up outlets to hit my sales targets.

I loved the Waikato and sport had been good to me and I talked to people about being involved in an organisation that promoted sport in the region. One person asked me why I hadn't mentioned Lion in our discussions. What he was showing me was that I needed to stop what I was doing, reflect and focus hard on what I was passionate about. That was life-changing for me.

Around 2001, I applied for a job advertised by Sport Waikato as a sponsorship manager. I spent a lot of time preparing for the interview and enjoyed the whole experience. Not long after, they told me I was not quite the person they wanted for that role, but they wanted me to come back to another interview with the board about possibly being chief executive of the organisation. As you could imagine, that offer came as a bolt out of the blue.

Sport Waikato was 15 years old then and had been without a CEO for six months. They had gone to the market a couple of times but failed to appoint anyone after John Parker then Murray Gutry had led the organisation. I spent the weekend mulling over many things. I was a real outsider for the job because I was effectively straight out of rugby and had little experience and had never led an organisation.

After being called back for a second interview, I began to

think maybe I had a shot, and they subsequently offered me the role.

There were mixed emotions of apprehension and immense pride and responsibility after the board showed their faith in me. That conviction was probably about Matthew Cooper the brand or Matthew Cooper the person and alignment to rugby as someone who could develop and grow with help from the experienced team at Sport Waikato.

I went through a four-week crash course in management in Mount Eliza, south of Melbourne, and tried to saturate myself in the tools I needed to lead an organisation. It was difficult because I was in charge of capable managers who'd been there for a long time and were very good at what they did and who had to deal with this new young ex-sportsman leading the group.

I took my time and listened a great deal to find out about the staff and used the principles I'd learned from my rugby career about being part of a team, preparing for a season, planning targets and goals and how to implement that in business and how that would work if someone was not pulling their weight. I could think back to times when you were a leader in rugby sides and how you'd deal with players who were not fully committed.

I linked back to the principles my wonderful parents instilled in me about believing in myself, using my common sense and treating people with respect. It doesn't matter what you do in life, you'll do okay if you live by those ideals.

There were lots of similarities in sport and business and that helped, but it has taken time and plenty of trial and error over the last 17 years to get the direction right. There are times when you have to make hard decisions that go against what the staff want, but I learned early that you can manage organisations — but managing is very different from leading them. The best interests of the organisation must always come first.

Sometimes you have to go through change to really understand what leadership is about, and in the last two or three years the organisation has seen plenty of change, and that has been quite defining in my career. There have been very good people involved along the way and Sport Waikato has delivered a number of successes.

Looking back, I was proud and daunted to be appointed and then the hard work started with gaining the breadth of understanding needed for the role. From being someone playing alongside teammates in a difficult test match or shield game, you went through the same things but as a leader of an organisation. When things are going well it is okay, but when the reverse is happening it can be a lonely position.

The key is to get good people and talk to good people.

In the early years it was hard not to take work home and that concerned me because my family is a very special part of me. My son Harrison works as a groundsman at St John's College and my daughter Grace is at Hillcrest High School, while my wife Kathryn is an outstanding mother and has a little business producing hand-made soap.

They are very important to me and number one in my life. You have to be careful about the boundaries and make sure your work–life balance is there.

My parents taught all of us about being resilient. The key thing for me is determination, and maybe that is my Croatian lineage, but that was the way I was brought up and the way I played my sport. I'm not brash, nor do I want to expose others and I believe conflict can be handled astutely and over time.

We had to be proud and learned to stand up for ourselves and to never undersell ourselves because everyone has a right to be treated the same way. There were some who were sceptical of my appointment, but I focused on being me rather than trying to be anyone else. I admit there are times when I don't know the answers, so I try to find out or happily defer to my excellent skilled staff.

Good communication and nurturing relationships, treating people how you like to be treated, valuing others' opinions and good dialogue are essential parts of running a business. A common-sense approach works, and I've developed a team that complements my skillset — and that's part of leadership.

I've learned a great deal and you get more philosophical as you get older. While it's a job, it is part of who I am, although with any luck no one is going to talk too much about me when I'm not here — hopefully more about the person.

Sport Waikato is a not-for-profit charitable trust that aims to break even annually and that's a challenging assignment. We are one of 14 regional sports trusts in New Zealand with a three-pronged strategic focus of growing participation, developing capability by improving sport, recreation and physical activity, and leading and enabling partnerships.

We have approximately 70 staff and we are funded by Sport New Zealand, the Waikato District Health Board, the Perry Group, Gallagher Engineering, Trust Waikato, 10 territorial authorities, philanthropic and gaming trusts and loyal long-term sponsors.

Under the new regional strategy for sport, recreation and physical activity that began in 2016, called Moving Waikato 2025, we will be working a lot closer with the public and communities in the Waikato region to grow participation numbers. We work closely with lots of organisations to develop their capability, to develop our coaches, administrators and volunteer base and we assist teachers by developing programmes that enhance the curricular spaces in schools.

Regional leadership is our last strategic pillar, which is about leading change from a sport, recreation and physical activity perspective alongside our key partners. We provide insight and data about facility planning, urban growth plans and regional strategies to capitalise on the Waikato's ever-growing high-performance framework to inspire our communities to get out there and be active.

Regional sports organisations like Waikato Rugby or Waikato/Bay of Plenty football are involved in the delivery, and Sport Waikato comes in behind to develop and support those organisations and their people.

Geographically, we are one of the larger sports trusts in New Zealand. Sport Waikato's boundaries include traditional rugby provincial areas like the King Country and Thames Valley and we go north to the Bombays with an increasing population currently sitting at about 430,000 in our region and somewhere around 70 per cent who live in or around Hamilton City.

Health funding is a major contributor at over 50 per cent of our total income, and the Waikato DHB understands the role of sport, recreation and physical activity in relation to health investment linked to prevention.

We want to cut out duplication of service, offer clarity of roles and reduce the overheads of providers so the funding dollar reaches the coal face and, most importantly, we want to listen and involve the communities, which is something I experienced in Canada earlier this year. They've got it; we need to understand it and it starts by trusting, listening and empowering our communities rather than by prescribing.

We have to be relevant for the future and a good example is our Waikato Regional Facilities plan from 2014 that identified and recommended two four-court indoor community courts rather than the traditional one large version.

Discussions started with potential partners like the new Rototuna High School, Wintec and the University of Waikato on their willingness to extend the Ministry of Education standard two-court model to a four-court competition-sized option that would significantly improve the annual costs around school use during the day and community use after school and on weekends. It's a smart model. Now we will target another four-court facility with interested parties at Wintec and the University of Waikato.

In our big move in 2016, Sport Waikato changed its structure and shifted our strategy with a mantra I use about respecting the past but being relevant for the future. Too many organisations stick to what they have always done and while I'm really big on history and there is a lot of that with Sport Waikato, we have to be relevant for the future.

Work can be very different each day and that's the exciting part about being the CEO, backed by great staff.

Away from my day job, I get requests to help out with goal-kickers, and for the last 17 years I've had the best seat in the house as part of Sky's commentary team for Super Rugby and provincial championship matches. It's a nice balance and a way of staying engaged in the game I still love.

My downtime is precious, and I make sure I look after myself so I'm still very big on fitness and was fortunate that in my 15-year first-class career, there were no significant injuries that have come back to bite me!

Working for Sport Waikato, the following should be unquestioned. We all need regular exercise for our health and well-being. It doesn't need to be a marathon or a two-hour gym workout every day — but to keep healthy, sharp and create a real perspective around balance, regular exercise is a must after a high-performance career.

CHRISTIAN CULLEN

A legendary attacking fullback, Christian Cullen represented New Zealand in 60 matches including 58 tests from his three-try debut against Samoa in 1996 until 2002. His 236 test points included 46 tries. In Super Rugby he played for the Hurricanes 1996–2003 and, at provincial level, Horowhenua, Manawatu, Central Vikings and Wellington. He also starred in the World Sevens competition and played for Munster in the Celtic League.

After the All Blacks, I had a final 2003 season with the Hurricanes and Wellington then went to Munster, which was both good and bad.

I travelled up there with a shoulder injury from my last game in New Zealand and was told it would be right, but when I arrived a scan showed a problem and they pretty much sent me straight to the operating theatre. It was not a good look, but the Irish kept me on with six months in rehab for the tear before I had a reasonably good stint, about 40-odd games on the trot and then did the other shoulder.

I think I was in Ireland for about four and a half seasons and played only half of that because of the shoulders, ankle, calf or something else.

The only silver lining was that I could still play golf. I couldn't lift my arms above my shoulder line, but I could swing a golf club, and the physios said if you can do that and not be in pain, then go for it. I did and played on some of the great courses. Ireland is a wonderful place with the villages and pubs if you want to go on holiday, like your golf and enjoy a few beers. It rains a lot, but if you are there for a month you can start down south and work your way up to Dublin or Belfast.

The best courses down in Cork were the Old Head of Kinsale, Adare Manor and the K Club and then a few nice ones up Belfast way, although we didn't manage to play there. You could take your pick in our area where they were a mix of links and parkland-type courses, while further up from Tralee there is Doonbeg and links-type courses right on the beach that are pretty cool.

I'd drive anywhere for golf. I lived in Cork and some of our golfing buddies were up in Limerick and they would have an hour's drive to Tralee and it would be two and a half hours' drive for me, but I'd say, 'See you there at nine.' I had the bug, which probably started with the All Blacks when we got some sponsored clubs.

My old man played, but when we were young golf wasn't the sport of choice. Now at our Paraparaumu club there are stacks of kids playing.

I'm not much of a tourist, to be fair. You see things a few times when you tour to the same places and don't need to visit them again, and playing golf instead was a great idea.

In Ireland I was into it and on single figures, but you needed to be careful with your handicap because money could change hands. I was dabbling, but it depended on how the day panned out. In New Zealand, it's different when you join a club and get a proper handicap.

It's a game which suited me with the walking and all sorts of mental stuff, and it's a respite from day-to-day life where the phone is off and you are with your mates. You can go anywhere in the world and there'll be different types of courses and we were lucky to have a smack on a lot of them.

You can only blame one person for what happens and there are those who blame the clubs, but it's actually the person holding them.

It got to the point where I came back from my final shoulder operation and I did my calf at training just through going up to catch a ball, landing a bit awkwardly and tweaking it. You come back from that then do an ankle, and I reached the stage where every morning I was waking up feeling sore and having to strap up and go to training then take it all off. I was thinking there is more to life than this.

I wasn't enjoying it any more. The games were cool, but I was over the training; I'd been doing it for a long time. In 2006 we came back home. I could have gone to Japan or France, but I thought I wanted to have a family and to be able to walk around a golf course when I'm 40 and play with the kids. You have to take it on the chin and say, 'Time's up, that'll do.'

When I came home I didn't know what I was going to do after rugby. I'd left school, worked at odd jobs as a stop-go man on the roads or for Fulton Hogan and played for my local footy team. Six months later, I went to Palmerston North and started a rugby development job with Manawatu Rugby going around schools then got into a sevens team and I was away.

My working life had been very short, so I never got a chance to sort out anything. When professional rugby started in 1996, though, we were paid well and I started buying rental properties and the like in Kapiti with my manager at the time, Dave Monnery. That was a start and we are still tight and co-own our property company.

When I came back from Ireland I had no idea what was in the future. I just wanted to come home and rest and get the body right. Even now, there are opportunities like working at Sky, which involves about 20 to 30 per cent of what I do, some property, and shares in the Four Kings bar in Wellington.

The funny thing in rugby is that you are in a bubble and people want to help you out. I was lucky to have my parents and Dave, but I know it has changed these days and the players get lots of advice. On the downside, when you retire there are people out there — sharks if you like — who you think are good buggers, but they are not.

I have invested in a few things and got burned, luckily not too badly, but you live and you learn.

A guy I went to do a deal with in Auckland ended up going to jail after I'd put a deposit down. I got all the lawyers' things signed up and the guy went bankrupt! That happens, but I am usually pretty careful about what I do.

Like rugby, you are always learning and you try to get good people around you. Every now and again you are going to make a mistake, but hopefully you don't make that same mistake twice. I have learned to do what you are good at and what you know — and for me that's the property game. I invested in bars with the proviso that I wasn't going to be there serving alcohol; I'm a silent partner.

I like the idea of development around Wellington and up the coast and having a relationship with a building company. I love living on the coast and there's a lot going on.

Another venture I looked at was a rugby video analysis system, which was an idea from Rob Neru who died a couple of years back. That was a yes and a no: it was a professional idea but more for the amateur player and only a few might have used it. We went to a lot of schools and some took it up; however, Rob wanted money to do more and we balked.

I have been pretty flexible and so when Sky approached me about commentaries with Super Rugby, All Blacks tours and the provincial championship, it suited and got me back into rugby.

There was a point where I had no interest in the game. There was a lot of kicking and rubbish, scrum resets and the like, so when they rang and asked I wasn't sure if it was for me. I never thought I would commentate, but it drags you back in, and you have to watch games and players and learn again.

It's been that sort of curve, as no one gives you any training and you are just thrown in there and wished good luck, but I've been lucky with Tony Johnson, Grant Nisbett and Scotty Stevenson who have been good to work with. You do it while it's there and see what happens.

You look at the papers and critique them, but when it comes to your turn with the questions and you are on TV and don't know the answer you have to make up something. I was told by Ken Laban, 'Stuff the questions; here's my answer,' and that's been quite useful advice to get me through some situations. There's the PC stuff and I'm not one to bag players or teams anyway; I don't want to do that. Then you are asked how a team can beat the All Blacks and you don't want to get too specific even when you think they can't.

I prefer being upstairs, as sideline work is tough. I'm no reporter and asking players questions is a hard gig. I take my hat off to Ian Smith down there; it's a different job, with a restricted view.

Some games are easier than others, and then there are the dull games or when you sound like a broken record talking about how teams are playing.

Away from that, I've got four kids under 10 who keep me busy, I'm in the property company with Dave Monnery, and I do some rugby promotions work, go to Hong Kong for the sevens each year and work at Sky most weeks.

I'm still looking for that something to go to two or three times a week, and that might take shape with the property company I'm dealing with. I enjoy taking the kids to school, picking them up then watching their cross-country or whatever sport they are into. My week hours are flexible, but the downside working with Sky is you can miss the kids' Saturday sport. I'd like to help out more, but it's hard to commit to the Tuesday, Thursday practice, Saturday game schedule because of my work.

Christian Cullen Management is involved in player and coach development. People can contact me through our website, while Dave Pollock runs my diary and sorts out the arrangements and the fees.

I like to keep fit and am regularly in the gym, but I wouldn't play now. There were a few games to help flood victims in Brisbane and matches for the Classics and my last game was about three years ago in the Cape Town tens, which was club-level stuff.

If you are not training, it is too easy to get an injury and be out for six months. My right knee has no cartilage, but I can do most things like tennis and golf. There will be a point, though, where I have to do something about it. These days they are doing all sorts of things we did not have access to such as growing cartilage and injecting it. Maybe in 10 years when I need something done there'll be something else.

If I ran every day my knee would swell up. Most days I do some cardio at the gym and some weights to help with my shoulders, and I eat well and don't drink much — not that I ever did. People are having heart attacks in their forties, and I'm at that age now. If I stop training, I lose weight, and I always wanted to get bigger.

Most Fridays we play golf. The funny thing is when you retire you make new sets of friends. I am the youngest of a bunch of local business guys who play in haggles and competition. My handicap is around three or four and I don't practise, but I could play every day and my knee would be okay if I used a cart.

I was invited to play in a tournament in Abu Dhabi with South African pro golfer Branden Grace. You get a bit of hope because you watch some of the pros and think there is not much to their game, but they are all awesome, particularly Dustin Johnson and Rickie Fowler who we managed to follow as well.

I was nervous with 15 people watching me tee off. It was a great experience being involved in the pro-am and we did okay, but what those pros do is so impressive. You can hit it as far as them, but they do it every shot. Grace was in the bunkers and got up and down all the time, while his caddy was awesome with the information he was giving him.

My local course, Paraparaumu, is always in good nick, but it's tough and every day can be different. I was brought up on the coast and Dane Coles is a capital coaster and Paul Steinmetz lives up the road.

I'm looking to the future more now with my kids and that's why I'm looking for something that can last because when you stop playing rugby the pay cheques stop as well. I try not to look back and ask 'What if?', and I want to give my two boys and two girls every opportunity. I don't yell and scream on the sidelines; I like to go behind the posts or sit quietly and watch. My oldest played rugby but is into swimming this year, while the girls cheerlead and do gym and the youngest boy loves getting out there with the rugby.

Fishing doesn't interest me; I don't enjoy it. Steiny always asks me to go out, but when the fish come up and start flapping around I feel sorry for them. If you're out there and not catching fish, you can't get off the boat.

I'm still restless looking for something that doesn't require 40 hours a week or wearing a suit or sitting behind a desk. As good as it is for me to be at home taking the kids to school and that sort of stuff, a mate of mine who owns a Pak 'n Save says it's good for the kids to see you go to work as well, instead of sitting around the house.

You see a few old mates at functions, but you make plenty of new friends. Sean Fitzpatrick was up there in Hong Kong several times and Zinzan Brooke was in Abu Dhabi and still competing. We take up where we left off and the rugby community has similar interests and gels quickly. As much as you hated each other on the field, most blokes are pretty cool off it.

I used to hate Springbok Mark Andrews on the rugby field and never socialised with him. I thought he was a prick. Then I turned up at Heathrow for a Baabaas game and the taxi sign said 'Cullen/Andrews', and we shared a cab and he was the best dude ever, very caring and considerate and a mongrel loose forward/lock. He was good to have on your team, just like George Gregan and Fitzy.

CRAIG DOWD

One of the most successful props of his era, Craig Dowd debuted in 1993 and was a front-row regular until 2000, most often with Sean Fitzpatrick (see later in this book) and Olo Brown. He represented New Zealand in 67 matches, including 60 tests, and scored two test tries. He played for the Blues in Super Rugby 1996–2001, as well as for Auckland, and made 115 appearances for London Wasps in the Guinness Premiership, 2001–2005.

Building was my business before professional rugby. As that life wound down, people were asking me what I was going to do, and those persistent enquiries weigh heavily on you and I'd turn around and say I hadn't any clue at all.

You run out of options, so the easy trick is to go into coaching because that's your game and you understand it, and if I'm expert at anything it's the technical aspects of scrummaging and knowing forward play. The thing about coaching, though, is you don't get much guidance or advice yourself.

Coaches follow their intuition and even these days are left to their own devices with few sounding boards. I was fortunate at Wasps in that I learned a great deal from the staff and then plenty from Ian McGeechan when he took over as the club's director of rugby.

My time there was very enjoyable, but about 10 years ago I felt it was time to stop being selfish and make the return to New Zealand — to put my family first. Initially, we thought we'd only be away for a couple of years, but life has a way of taking you down new paths.

One of those was an opportunity that cropped up as rugby development manager for North Harbour and involved running the academy and looking after young players. Geographically, the job suited us as a family living on that side of the bridge, so I put my hand up and got the job, which gave me something to come home to. We sold our house in London, bought back in Auckland and came home.

My last game of rugby for Wasps was a couple of months before my thirty-sixth birthday.

My body had been creaking for a while and I'd also done my Achilles, and if I hadn't sorted that out in six months the club was going to terminate my contract. They were probably looking at that anyway, so I went through a rehab programme where I cut holes in the cast to attach electrodes to the damaged area to keep the muscles working. I did everything to get it right because it was my last chance as a player to earn really good money.

Eventually, I got back on the field five months and one week later and saw out the season.

My final match was at Twickenham in 2005 when we beat Leicester in the Premiership final. It was supposed to be their day and Martin Johnson's big hurrah, but it was my farewell too, so I was determined to finish strongly. It was a fantastic way to hang up my boots in front of a full house of 82,000 people with a trophy in the cabinet.

That was about eight years after my last All Blacks test and I'd begun doing a bit of coaching at Wasps where I had a really good relationship with Warren Gatland, Tony Hanks and Shaun Edwards on the staff.

Part of the reason I stayed was to mentor the next players coming through and help out with the academy and the A team where they blooded all the young talent. That work gave all of us ideas about coaching, mentoring and where life might take us after we stopped playing. It was a useful transition because you can't go straight from playing to coaching and do it seamlessly; you make so many mistakes.

Six months after moving as a player to a coaching role I was still getting involved in some of the trainings, and that was not a good look. There was one defining moment in a contact session where I landed an elbow or shoulder on a player's nose and there was plenty of blood and all the players looked up and wondered what had gone on. If another player had been involved that would have been okay, but it was different when the coach did it to a player.

I was supposed to be building confidence in them rather than taking it away, so I made a vow to never get involved in another contact session. As a coach you need to be removed to oversee what's happening rather than showing them how it should be done.

The turning point for our move came as my contract was coming up for renewal and my daughter Georgia was about to go to secondary school. If I had signed on again, it would have been for another two years, and at that stage she would have been well into school life and it would have been unfair to rip her away from all her friends if we then wanted to move.

We'd been away about eight years and had had a good time, we'd bought a house in Ealing in London and life was pretty good, but we missed New Zealand.

My job at Harbour involved identifying talent and reporting to New Zealand Rugby, which was a huge change from the very insulated club scene in England. We had two teams at Wasps and that was it, and whatever happened inside those walls stayed there, while in New Zealand there is so much more information shared.

Amateur club rugby standards here had dropped back to the level of senior reserves when I was playing here in the 80s and 90s, but schoolboy rugby was terrific, while all the talent was being sucked in the direction of professional rugby. That was interesting because I came back with a mindset that club and community rugby should come first. If you look at why anyone would get involved in rugby, it's not always about being a professional, it's about playing with your mates, keeping fit and having fun.

After a year back home, North Harbour coach Wayne Pivac moved on to another role and I graduated to the provincial job. It wasn't something I was looking for, I didn't seek it, but the job came looking for me and fell in my lap. I knew I didn't need to rush into coaching because as soon as you put your hand up for the top coaching role you are much more in the firing line.

In hindsight, I wasn't ready for the job and I didn't enjoy it. If I wanted to be a career coach I needed a 20-year plan because you are putting all your eggs in one basket and you're not looking to move into some other role afterwards. When it finishes, that's it.

However, I put my hand up, took on the Harbour job and really hated it.

We had some good results, but it wasn't enjoyable. The union has a small base of rugby numbers and you are always under the microscope from a very intelligent community with lots of high-powered individuals where everyone is expecting success.

In two years I think we won four games each year. In the first season, most matches were relatively close then in the next we had some horrible results, so when the union asked me to do a review and reapply I declined. It didn't work for me. I told them they should either have full confidence in me or not and asking me to reapply showed they had some doubts.

I looked at our results and said to them, 'If I was in your position, I'd sack myself,' so rather than choose to reapply I decided to walk. I'm the sort of person who thinks that if you are going to do a job, you do it properly and you try to be successful, but if it doesn't work out and you are not successful, you should get out and do something else.

At that point I was exhausted and mentally drained by the whole coaching experience and felt I was on the verge of something more sinister, so I had to get away for my own mental health. I thought I'd take time out and wait until I found the right thing for me.

Throughout that tough period, I'd also been struggling with my hearing and it got to the point where I couldn't hear conversations with people who spoke softly or in crowded atmospheres where there was a lot of high-pitched noise.

I found myself asking people to repeat themselves and

would try to lip-read or often nod my head, pretending I'd heard them. I became withdrawn and paranoid, doubting myself, and I relied heavily on my close support crew.

Eventually, I went and got tested and discovered I had lost 60 per cent of my hearing.

My father-in law gave me his spare set of hearing aids and it was the most amazing difference to hear birds, crickets and all sorts of high-pitched noises. All those sounds came back, and it was incredible.

Hearing aids have restored my confidence and communication and other parts of my life have all improved — now I need to sort my eyes out and slow this ageing process down!

At the end of my time at Harbour, my wife and kids were on tenterhooks around me. That was the real crunch because I knew that through coaching I had turned into someone who was not working for my family. You want to pick up a ball or play with your kids, but that family time evaporates because you are so focused on what should happen in your job.

The success of a week depends on what happens in 80 minutes of rugby and that could come down to one missed penalty. I remember one game, in the last minute we had a penalty to win and Mike Harris hit the post and the ball bounced away. Those moments are coach-killers — you are torn up and carry all the burdens.

Too many coaches have been and gone at Harbour and there must be more to that pattern. I take a helicopter view of it now and believe some of the ideas I brought in worked and had the union heading in the right direction before other coaches arrived and did it their way.

Harbour's forwards were always very competitive with solid set-piece work, so the base of the game was there, and on our day, we could have beaten most teams. However, there is a warning for players going into coaching that it is not all it's cracked up to be, and it is not playing; it is entirely different.

If I had my chance again, I would look at a completely different career path. Beginning as an assistant in the UK and starting here as an assistant is completely different from being a head coach. You lose your sense of humour, you become withdrawn and I wanted to get my fun back and be the character I knew I was.

Walking away was the best part for all of us, my wife Tanya, our daughter Georgia who has been to her second year at Camp America and our boy Billy who is the skinniest tighthead prop in the First XV at Long Bay College.

After six or seven months' downtime, I still felt I was unemployable. I didn't want to go back to building, not with a broken-down body. In my first year after retiring I had to bump my way down the stairs on my arse because I had to warm up my lower back and crook ankle for an hour before I could walk properly. It took about a year for that to come right.

While coaching Harbour was tough, I met some really good people including Carey Burt who is now my business partner at d3 tape. He was involved with QBE Insurance and crazy about rugby and we got talking about our boys who are a similar age and tackle techniques and how it would be great if they each owned a bag.

We talked about how those bags should look for guys of a certain size and age, so we made them about 330 millimetres wide and 1200 high with a foam core that would bounce once you hit it. Barfoot & Thompson loved it, Rebel Sport did too, and that was really the impetus for this d3 company.

We made such a great tackle bag that once a customer

walked away with one you'd never see them again. We kept talking about ideas, and one night Carey and I were watching our daughters play netball and I told him how I couldn't believe we spent about $14,000 on strapping tape at Harbour.

Every Saturday you'd see players put all this tape on then after the game the manager would be sweeping it all up and chucking it in the bin. That happened after every training and every game. When I was young, I'd walk past the 3M tape company in New Lynn and think I'd love to have a dollar for every roll of tape they sell and that resonated with me so we started up the d3 (Three Dads) company.

We took 12 months touring around the country, talking to companies, physios and finding the right quality of tape. Once we sorted that, we had to find points of difference with sizes, volume, colours and price and then get the packaging right.

We made an early call that we were getting a bit top-heavy with rugby emphasis and we didn't want to be known solely as a rugby tape. For the first few years, we used my profile to get the product out there then we had Sarah Cowley, the heptathlete, help us connect with our other target areas.

We supply everyone from the very young to pensioners who need to strap their knees and it's for those playing sport, anyone returning from injury or wanting to get back in the garden. We wanted it to be available to everyone, so we had to be retail savvy and look for price points and volume. Now we are available throughout New Zealand and Australia and have set our sights further afield to work alongside retailers and for the product to sit beside everyday needs in the supermarket.

At the start, we had a three-year plan that has taken double that time. Our motto was survive then grow and dominate.

Going home after work now is the greatest thing and being

happy in your family life is gold. It's not till you get away from a bad environment and get your head clear that you realise what you've been through.

It's still stressful when you have to make enormous decisions around your business, but it's different. I look at our products and have self-belief about selling them.

Our policy is about offering good-quality value where our margins are small so making big decisions is a minimal risk. We learned a big lesson in 2014 about margins and exchange rates, so we've now employed a strong accounting person, Stephen Burt, with experience in merchant banking and finance.

After leaving Harbour, I did some work for Sky at a time when most of the guests were backs, so there was not as much emphasis on forward areas and a great deal of silence around scrums. That work gave me the best seat in the house, but I am not a talkative person by nature; I like to think and ponder about things while the audience wants to hear something straight away.

Eventually, working at Sky and starting up the business became too busy, so I decided to limit my involvement to provincial rugby. Coaching helped me become more articulate and to mature as a person and I do the odd thing on radio and write a regular column on ESPN that offers me an outlet for my passionate opinions on things like concussion and injury.

My motivation is to help educate the next generation. In my spare time, I watch games that interest me, but I don't get too emotional about it all. I don't see many of my old playing mates, but when I do, we quickly get back on the same wavelength.

Fishing and boating are my big passions away from work and I've got a big trailer boat, a McLay 680, but these days I only go out in good weather looking for snapper or diving with my son. We can do that together as equals, hunting crays or finding scallops.

My life is far more balanced now and I get great enjoyment from my work then relaxing with my family and having one of my wife's fantastic meals — her Indian food is outstanding — which all helps me be in the best space I've been for a long time.

SEAN FITZPATRICK

Sean Fitzpatrick is one of the best-known players of the modern era. He debuted in 1986 as hooker and later that year began an unbroken run of 63 tests, with 92 tests overall, including as captain from 1992 until 1997, and bagged 12 test tries. He appeared for the Blues in Super Rugby 1996–97, and for Auckland 1984–97.

When I was 28 and the All Blacks had won the first World Cup then lost the next, I was thinking about retiring. My wife Bronnie and I spoke about it a lot. I'd experienced success and failure at the event and had always worked in some capacity as a builder and the construction game suited me.

I loved the development side of that business and I also got involved with Coca-Cola. I suppose we were lucky because we always worked and knew there was more to life than just playing rugby. In 1991 I thought that would be it, but then, courtesy of one Laurie Mains, my career took off again really and the second half was probably better than the first part.

I kept working and once more considered giving the game

away after the 1995 World Cup, but the excitement and opportunity of leading that team to South Africa kept me going. By then Bronnie and I had bought and sold a couple of houses and we enjoyed that challenge, and then 1997 came along and my wonky knee forced me into retirement.

It wasn't easy to let go of the game I loved and a lifestyle that was so much a part of me, but I suppose there's the fear of failure in terms of leadership and questions about what you are going to do next. However, I think I knew what I wanted to do and that evolved steadily.

A number of times, I sat down with Kevin Roberts who helped map out where I should be going and who I should be associated with in terms of companies and brands, so we had the Coca-Cola business, a bit of property building and then I was lucky enough to continue working for New Zealand Rugby for a couple of years.

I wasn't doing stacks of work on the tools, but we always had a house project on the go, and I liked to be involved and had several very interesting builds in Remuera in Victoria Avenue and Arney Crescent. Towards the end, I was involved more in the operational side of things, getting plans organised and managing the construction.

I let things develop, really. I have never been one with a long-term vision. We both liked work and while I had my rugby and construction, Bronnie was working as a lawyer and we had an enthusiasm to work hard, so it was never about sitting back. There was never a case of sitting down with a 10-year plan and saying, 'This is what we are going to do, these are our targets, and this is how we are going to get there.'

When my playing days were done, I enjoyed staying connected to rugby, managing the New Zealand Colts with

Richie McCaw, Dan Carter and all those guys. It was a change of lifestyle because playing for the All Blacks is such a commitment and having the time to do other things was exciting.

Even when we both turned 40 and decided to head away to Europe for two years, it was quite an out-there thing for us to sell everything at home, put our kids, Grace and Eva, in the back of the car and go travelling without any certainty of a job.

We treated the trip to Europe as an adventure rather than an escape from the goldfish bowl of attention in New Zealand. I have never had an issue with that. Travelling was an opportunity, and we termed it as an OE because we had never done that trip, which so many Kiwis do, other than tacking on holidays after end-of-year rugby tours. We wanted to experience Europe and all that it could offer, and we were lucky we could do it and that there was enough work and I had an Irish passport that allowed access to the European Union.

At the start, there was some work in television and hospitality before the World Cup in 2003, and the victory for England gave rugby a real boost in Europe. It was great to get an opportunity to get into some television work, which gave me more exposure and profile and helped me branch out to other things.

Once we worked out the direction of the sun and that people needed south-facing properties, we dipped our toes into that market again and set up a company and went through all the groundwork to get that up and running. They were issues I hadn't encountered before, but Bronnie's father was an accountant and having him and a lawyer wife was a very good foundation for our plans.

The Front Row Group started through meeting people and revving up the hospitality work. We met a guy who said he would like to use us and so did different clients of ours, and, once again, we didn't really know how we were going to do that. It evolved, a typical Kiwi thing I guess, mixed in with an attitude of not being afraid to try and hooking into it.

At that time, opportunities increased because England had won the World Cup and that created all sorts of areas of interest including corporate hospitality.

I found the most challenging thing in Britain was the scale of everything because there might be a thousand people doing the same thing we were. You have to be better than them, and being a former All Black didn't give you any advantages or rights of access.

It all happened through trial and error probably, meeting the right people, having the right contacts and having the right advisors, associating yourself with the right people — and I think we have always been quite careful about that.

Everything we do we try to enjoy it. You have to make sure you enjoy people, especially in the hospitality side where we're being ambassadors and out in the public arena a lot.

Much of what I learned came from family values, and as long as I remained true to those principles in my work and daily life I'd advance. Up in Europe, if you piss somebody off, there is always someone to take your place very quickly in this huge market.

I find it all very rewarding. Nowadays I do a lot more speaking and spend time with my children, which in the early days wasn't so much the case. I suppose it has been all about the opportunities that we have been given through playing the game.

I especially like the business audiences because with the All Blacks being so successful at the moment and continuing the great traditions that have built up over 100 years and more, audiences are really engaged and like to use sport as a metaphor to enhance their businesses.

Basically, I show business people how they can apply the principles in sport to whatever work they are involved in. A lot of the people don't even know the All Blacks, and they definitely don't know me, but they understand the analogies between sport and business.

I work on it. When I speak to industries I try to connect sport's principles to the line of business they are in. One of the great spin-offs has been learning about a whole lot of different enterprises that I never would have had much idea of or connection with before — but each experience is interesting and gives you a broader outlook on life.

I'm on the board at Harlequins rugby club, which links me to the game in Europe and keeps me in contact with the action side of things. We've had our challenges. Club rugby is big business, but there can be issues with players because they are not centrally contracted as they are in New Zealand.

I go to most of the Quins' home games out at the Stoop, and Michael Lynagh and I commentate on most of the southern hemisphere rugby that Sky in the UK has access to. We go into the station every weekend to cover two or three games that are shown live up here, but we only have a studio for Saturday morning. When the All Blacks play up here we follow them around everywhere from Ireland to Italy and France.

Our host presenter is James Gemmell who used to work in New Zealand and is the son of former All Black Bruce. It's great and I enjoy it and it's something Michael and I have done since 1999 with the icing every four years when we have the World Cup and Sky releases us to work for ITV.

I'm also chairman of the Laureus World Sports Academy and vice-chair of the Laureus Sports Foundation, which is probably the thing I have enjoyed most in recent times. It is a great honour. I remember sitting down with them for the first time in Monaco 17 years ago and thinking, 'What am I doing here amongst all these great athletes?', and now to be involved is an incredible thrill. In my early days, Tiger Woods or Roger Federer was winning the annual awards.

The foundation's work throughout the year is growing, which is what most of us do it for. We support about 120 charities with a sporting component to them and the interests of children. We don't have our own projects but have connections to charities in about 35 countries. It is amazing and very special, and we distribute about eight or nine million euros a year.

Early on, I went to Sierra Leone, which changed my life and reinforced how lucky we really are. I had never had any contact with anything to do with civil war. It is such a cruel form of combat where brothers and sisters are woken in the middle of the night and threatened they will have their hands cut off if they don't go to war.

I was there in 2004 with Tony Hawk, the champion skateboarder, to front the Right to Play project, which aimed to help those children who were forced to kill each other to remember and reconnect with their childhood by playing games.

Neither of us had seen anything like it; the place was in ruins. The buildings were smashed, there was rubbish everywhere and it was chaotic, but Tony went through his skating tricks and we played around with rugby balls to try to help teach them to be kids again. It almost seemed a futile gesture, but it was a start for those poor kids and so much better than what they had been through.

They loved the way Tony made his skateboard dance and they also loved a haka I did and responded with a few dances themselves.

Another visit I made with Laureus was to a school in Rajasthan, India where children who were affected by polio became involved in sport and won medals at the Paralympic Games and used that message to help change perceptions of disabilities. It was really wonderful seeing the change in attitudes and direction in life.

We are also involved in the Fight for Peace in the favelas in Rio where the young people face a multitude of issues because of the decades of drug-related violence.

An amazing young English guy, Luke Dowdney, started the initiative in 2000 and set up a boxing organisation where the children of warring families meet halfway and box, as a way of breaking down the tensions in the favelas. It is a phenomenal project and his work has received wide recognition.

Fight for Peace is based on boxing and martial arts, and it embraces a holistic approach for its pupils who learn about community investment and education to help them with employment.

We have also supported the Urban Stars project in West Belfast since 2011, which aims to break down barriers and reduce tension between Catholics and Protestants by giving them tools to help their lives. The idea is to break down the crime rates and alter the behaviour of teenagers by offering them coaching in boxing, football, basketball, weightlifting, dance and group sessions to help channel their development.

In late 2016, I travelled to Grenada in the Caribbean where we have an amazing project called the Homeless World Cup, run by a former Premiership footballer who was brought up in the East End of London and was involved in community activities there and went back to Grenada and asked us to support his idea. It is a five-a-side football competition for those who live on the streets and they get a chance to go to a global tournament.

We started a Youth in Action initiative there and my trip coincided with a visit from Prince Harry when we announced a partnership of projects on the island to improve the lives of children in the Caribbean.

Volunteers running that programme are players who represented Grenada at the Homeless World Cup tournaments in Amsterdam and Glasgow. Laureus has more plans to assist disadvantaged children on the island and throughout the Caribbean, which shows the powerful messages sport can provide.

NORM HEWITT

Hooker Norm Hewitt represented New Zealand in 1993 and 1995–98, playing in nine tests and scoring seven tries, but he was reserve to Sean Fitzpatrick in 38 tests. He played with the Hurricanes in Super Rugby 1992–2001, and represented Hawke's Bay, Southland and Wellington.

My rugby came to a halt midway through the provincial championship in 2001. I was Wellington captain but still injured and I walked into the dressing room and said, 'Guys, I'm out and I'm finished. I wish you all the best.' I knew in my heart I wasn't living up to my expectations or those of the team. I shook all their hands and that was it.

The end had been gradual. I played with a broken arm that hadn't set properly for a year and I was in so much pain every morning that mentally I wasn't in a good space. I was playing for the livelihood more than the game. My interest was waning. There was no final game where the crowd cheered and all that sort of stuff.

When players come to the end of their careers many don't know when to stop and I wanted to have control of that space. That was it and no one from the rugby union rang to find out what was happening.

My body was sore, and it was no longer enjoyable. It just wasn't worth carrying on. At the start of the year, I was told I wouldn't be in the Hurricanes and wasn't one of the top 15 hookers in the country and there was a whole lot of politics going on, so I finished and thought 'Holy crap, what am I going to do?'

I stared out the window . . . I had no skills, no qualifications, what do I do? I was lucky to have a good mentor at the time, Ray Thompson, who runs the Cloud 9 Foundation for children with Asperger's syndrome, and he asked me how much money I needed to live on. I told him, and he paid me that to work for him.

Six months later, he said, 'I'm firing you today because you'll be fine.'

Not long after, I was at an event in Lower Hutt when I was tapped on the shoulder by Roger McClay, who was then Children's Commissioner, and I became an ambassador for several years, travelling the country in an advocacy role on behalf of vulnerable children. That was coincidence, and from then on I have been a great believer in every moment being an opportunity.

I was doing all sorts, but the first priority was to take care of home, take care of the family.

Before I finished rugby, I knew I had to connect with people, but I came with some baggage and that was the hindrance. I set some goals in talking with a friend of mine, Dean Eagar, and went out to achieve them.

I wanted to work for three companies, Air New Zealand, the New Zealand Army and some charity work with the SPCA. I needed a car and ran some tours for a company and was involved in radio commentary on rugby and a bit for Sky, so there was enough to keep me going.

It was the continuation of the journey. My drinking episode in Queenstown in 1999 was the catalyst for change and an abrupt and necessary shock. From then on it was about discovering who I was, and the start of humility and developing myself as a man.

The Commissioner put me on the right pathway and when I read reports on Lillybing, James Whakaruru, the Aplin sisters and Coral Burrows — all children who had died at the hands of adults — they staggered me. There would be a beautiful picture of a child's face, a name and date of birth and death and we'd wait for some recommendation. Then there'd be another report and that cycle continued. There were boxes from floor to ceiling of reports about kids, and I could have been one of those statistics and was still on that path of being one. Queenstown was a reflection of the turmoil in my life and what I now describe as the day I was trapped in prison from the age of nine, due to violation by my father.

In 2003 I got married. It was very significant. Arlene was working at Bodyworks where we all trained and her mutual friend introduced us and we had just started seeing each other when Queenstown happened. I told her she needed to get out of that space, but she said she saw something in me.

There was a moment that I call 'living with angels' when she gave me a hug. I promised her I would never behave like that again, and I had to go on a journey of self-discovery to do that. I went back to a marae, caught up with two of my best mates who helped me, went to Tauranga where I met Herewini Jones who helped put pieces together about where I come from, who I am and what it all means.

Then it was about understanding that I have the power to change whatever I want but that I need the tools to do so. I didn't need to be given the tools; I needed to be shown how to use them.

Arlene has been a rock for me because I had sabotaged all my previous relationships when I did not live in a world of calmness, as I felt better in a world of chaos. Instead of manning up and saying this is not working, I would create the chaos to destroy it.

But I became ready and open and willing to accept our relationship, and that is a hugely important thread.

Arlene is the boss. I keep thinking I am, and I am an intense person like most who have been in a high-performance arena, but she was too, so there was this equality and now our whole devotion is our kids — Elizabeth who is 13 and Alexander who is 11. Arlene is my angel, my pou, which is the central pillar in a meeting house that goes so deep you can't move it.

When Roger McLay's term as Children's Commissioner ended, so did my advocacy job, so a friend suggested I call Celia Lashlie. I went to see her and had a cup of tea — all my philosophy is based on that cup of tea, about 10 years ago. What an amazing wahine. Trevor Grice, founder of Life Education Trust, was also there, and I just wanted to get out there and work for those two.

We had a bare bones idea about social fabric being based around a school and every community connecting with that school and soon we were sitting in a bank asking for $10 million. We drew a picture where the hub is the school with concentric circles showing relationships, where there are holes and where there is nothing at all. Our job was to strengthen those relationships and reconnect people into the school. The bank people said they'd give us $250,000, no strings attached.

We did that work for about eight years, walking across New Zealand into communities and saying, 'We are not here to tell you what to do; what would you like us to do?' I was the apprentice and learnt a lot from absorbing some of Celia and Trevor's wealth of knowledge.

In the middle of that, I was involved in the TV show *Dancing with the Stars*, which lifted our profile and support around the country. However, every year became more about justifying funds and we'd get $20 and spend $15 justifying it and have $5 left over for charity, so in the end it was better to cool it and we closed the trusts.

We refined it to the hub of the school, and in my last couple of years Trevor had retired and Celia wanted to go down her track of helping women who'd been in prison. There were problems with adults' behaviour and the kids were losing out because of it, and it felt like everyone was positioning themselves for what's in it for me; it was about ego and that was unacceptable.

My work with the SPCA was bubbling along, talking to Year 7 and 8 kids about pets being part of the family. I grew up with a horse, a dog and a cat, and at times they were my greatest friends and my refuge when it was time to cry because they didn't answer back and had unconditional love.

I didn't realise how many young people did the same thing.

I recall many years ago the All Blacks playing in the UK in the middle of our night. The old man goes down the road to get our fish and chips and comes back seven hours later and they are cold, so he puts them in the oven to heat and we tune up the black-and-white TV. Andy Dalton was captain and from that moment I knew I was going to be an All Black, so I talk about living the dream, but when the violation happened everything changed.

Then I did become an All Black and I didn't like who I had become — someone I hated. I was never that person when I was a boy, but environment, circumstance and choices had all come into play.

Along the way, I saw the behaviour of the staffroom set the culture of the classroom.

About five years ago, I was at Rangikura primary school in Porirua and asked the principal if I could work with the school to set up a pilot programme across two or three years building the capacity of leadership and conversations in the staffroom around changing their behaviour to have an effect in the classroom.

Teachers would say, 'Do as I say not as I do,' and kids could see the conflict between teachers who were telling the kids to sort the conflict out amongst themselves. We were getting teachers chastising kids but not looking at themselves, and that's a fundamental human flaw.

I needed champions. I told them they all had to apologise to the kids for broken relationships and when they said they wouldn't, I said I was out. It was time for a chat and more cups of tea to try to do what was best for the kids.

I'd watch the staff sitting at their laptops, looking at their phones or their watch or doing something else while I was talking and all working independently of each other. There was no collective interaction and I was asking how this helped kids learn. We started father–son breakfasts and movie nights, mother–daughter pampering days and getting the teachers to greet the kids every morning. Then there was a cup of tea meeting between them all.

It was changing teachers' behaviour as much as children's. At one time, they'd say, 'Sorry, that's teacher's chair,' and I'd say, 'Thank you for making me feel welcome with that hierarchical power stuff.' Who are the most influential daily forces with children? It's the teachers.

Out of 400 kids and 100-plus parents, about 10 per cent of parents turned up to initial parent–teacher interviews, but within 18 months we got 97 per cent attendance because the attitude of the teachers had changed, and the kids started to care and told their parents and said, 'Our school is great; we love going there.'

There are stacks of kids who can identify with what I've been through and can see where I am now and want to change. That transfer of heart is the whole premise of my work, so when I am teaching the teachers I say it is the exchange of heart before information. If you don't capture the heart, you cannot capture the head.

Who has the greater wisdom, the teacher or the kid?

There's no point in ringing a parent and saying, 'Norm has been a little shit today, come and get him,' because the parent will think you are attacking them and will be defensive. Instead we need to talk, but the fear of teachers is high, and they need to give time and conversation.

These principles run through all my work these days with fund groups or management groups in Australia to mentoring managers at Air New Zealand to demolition contractors — and it is all about talk and the culture of a company. That culture is based on people and if they don't have a voice, how do they grow?

Leadership enables culture and if the chief executive is not on the wavelength, is not engaged or blames middle management, it's a waste of time. I'll tell the CEO that he contradicts every rule he has made when he says he's the boss, it's his right, he's earned his stripes or it is the way he was taught.

When a teacher tells a kid that the class would be better off without him, I say, 'Seriously, you just ripped the heart out of that child in front of his mates.' Teachers say they have to deliver the curriculum and don't have time to deal with kids with all this baggage who don't want to learn anyway.

But I am saying that when the kid comes in and shakes the teacher's hand and says I'm sorry for throwing that chair, and the student goes clean slate and the teacher says, 'Bet he does it again tomorrow,' he's just set up the kid to fail.

Teachers have a massive workload, are not paid well and of course need to have a home life. I would do whatever it takes to keep the good ones, but there are teachers who are stealing the futures away from kids. They talk the language of 'kids in, kids out'. There are some who don't care and who hate kids. Why are they doing it?

The All Blacks can select the best of the crop; why can't we have that at school too instead of just having an academic pass standard? Teachers are so important because they spend so much time with our kids and we are not giving them the tools. Teachers begin to internalise everything.

Their work is a calling, a sort of educational mission.

A company I visited last year had 50 per cent of their staff fail a drugs test, but this year they've had a clean slate because they all came on the journey. It is a continuum and there are still disruptions, but the staff have been encouraged and sorted out and everyone understands each other's circumstances.

Where's my life going? It could be anywhere. I am part of a group working with men coming out of prison. John Wareham, who worked in Rikers Island prison in New York, is teaching me about philosophy and the way men work, and I'd like to do more work with inmates and the Department of Corrections.

Now I'm speaking a lot with my father and ask him what I'm going to say at his funeral. Am I going to talk about this angry man who beat us or am I going to talk about someone who broke the cycle and owned the space — that's the man I want to talk about. We went to rugby one afternoon to watch my boy play and he said he understood it, and that was a revelation.

My life will unfold.

I'm here to change the world. It is the missionary part of me because every time I'm with men or a group who cry and say thank you, there is a reward. Families are waiting for their men to come home and be men, and when young boys have forgotten what their journey to manhood looks like, we have to put help their way.

The work is draining, but I don't carry the weight or worry with me any more.

I'm a way better father and nurturer at home to my kids. I am becoming more lateral in my thinking, and I'm not the dictator any more like my father was. I'll say, 'I think you can make a better choice,' or 'Let's talk about how you want to do it,' and that's a recent thing and we are working on it. I want to work on ways of making my son and daughter the greatest people in the world without pressuring them along those lines. It should happen naturally.

I want to put a measure on it and on the day I die, others can do that. As Muhammad Ali said, 'If a man of 50 is still thinking the way he did things at 20, then he has wasted 30 years of his life.' I want to be a good man.

ANDREW HORE

Andrew Hore debuted for the All Blacks as hooker on the northern hemisphere tour in 2002 and became an integral member of the team until 2013, playing 83 tests and scoring eight tries. He played for the Crusaders, Hurricanes and Highlanders in Super Rugby, and represented Otago, Taranaki and Southland.

The biggest problem young guys have now is speaking to people, having an interview like this because they sit down, put their heads down and start texting. You can't go to the pub and have a yarn because they are all on their phones. We used to have team dinners, but there would be 10 people on their phones, and our hardest job was getting them to meet and greet people.

That's how it is, though. They've done nothing different since school and that's the modern environment. You don't even have to talk to a woman either, you just text her and the job's done, and that might have served some of us ugly buggers better, but never mind.

When I left school, I was always going back to the farm; there was never any doubt about that. I suppose that was the reason I had to leave Otago because I reached their standards through natural ability and staying on the farm instead of going to town and the gym.

It wasn't until I went to Taranaki and the farm was miles away that I was forced to get into the gym much more. Being on the farm was awesome, but to get from a naturally fit footy player to the next level where you get pushed more was a case of changing from a part-time player to a fully concentrated locked-in footy player. It still wasn't quite full-time in Taranaki because we only trained Mondays and Tuesdays.

The easy part for me was when I thought I'd had enough rugby the farm was there; that was always going to be my life. Anton Oliver played the last few years because he didn't know what his next chapter was going to be, but I always had that certainty. I enjoyed the money, but I wasn't playing rugby to make money, I wasn't going to go overseas to play for a club that meant nothing to me, although it could be a big mistake now that I'm paying the bills.

The reality is I'm similar to an old-style player who loved farming and regarded time off as farm time. I'm a much more contented soul there. It is where you grow up and what you know, and I was good at it because I didn't enjoy the school side of things too much.

The old man never pressured me to come back to the farm, which has been in the family for more than a century and five generations. He never asked about rugby unless you wanted to discuss it and the same with farming, so it was enjoyable going out with him and learning stuff by being around him, watching and listening. There was never any conversation about whether you are coming home to farm — probably the opposite.

In 2000 when I went up to Taranaki I talked to him about going back to farming instead of playing rugby and he told me I was silly and to play all the footy I could.

My brother Charlie and I are in the process of splitting up the property, which is roughly two hours from Dunedin and two hours from Queenstown, because we bought the neighbour's farm, so he'll get that and my wife Frankie and I will get the home place.

We run sheep and beef on the farm and before we split it we did about 13,500 ewes lambing, 500 cows to the bull and 5000 hoggets, 3000 wethers and we fattened a few steers. So it's a big operation, and this year's been good with wool and beef prices going through the roof. There's no cropping, only winter feed, and 90 per cent of the wool goes out on contract with Radar and Icebreaker clothing.

We are set up for merinos because of the dry climate for wool and their lambs, and then beef for the hill country. We are understocked on about 46,000 acres, but when it's split Frankie and I will have about 26,000 acres and that'll be good, and the old man can live here until he's in a box.

We're also at the start of the Maniototo irrigation scheme and have 1000 acres irrigated that is gravity-fed, so when it is dry we are still guaranteed hay. Around Central you are either too dry or it rains. Growing up in the area helps you understand it; if you came down from up north to farm, it would be tougher.

We are not going to diversify — that's like going to England and playing for money — wool is our business, not dairying. We might get our B&B business going some more; we'll see. It's still pretty laid back around here where you can go to footy, which is about 20 minutes' drive from home, and leave your car unlocked.

It's home and it wasn't until Frankie came down and started talking about all the great views and the scenery that you realise how lucky you are to live there.

Like any job there are parts of it you prefer more than others, but as long as the family is fine and Frankie is up to speed with the bookwork then we're good. I'm not afraid of it, but it's not my thing. Frankie is not going to go to the bull sale to pick out the best bull, but she can write up the paperwork and ride the horses. I'm more into the stockman side of things. We don't do a lot of tractor work and we get contractors in to do the ploughing. I'm not a real machinery sort of person, but I feed out hay in the winter and use the quad bike.

We do all the mustering on horses, so in April we help with some syndicate mustering where we spend weeks staying in huts and getting the sheep in. We go to the neighbour's place first where there are no fences and stay out for four nights in the huts.

The cooks come out with the tucker and the huts sleep 12 with a coal-range at one end and a potbelly at the other and are insulated — quite a change from sleeping under a tin roof and cutting tussock for your bed like they used to. The old man is building a new hut on our property which was going to be made from second-hand iron, but it's now Colorsteel and includes double-glazed windows.

At the end of 2013, I came back into farming full-time. I'd sort of had enough and didn't think I would make it to the 2015 World Cup. I fought with Keven Mealamu and Anton Oliver to get starts then on the way down another good kid, Dane Coles, came along who is bloody handy. We had a meeting about how long we were going to play and Kevvie was adamant he wanted to make it to 2015. I wasn't going to get a Highlanders contract again so thought that would do me as far as rugby goes.

I was old school when they asked me about the World Cup. I felt there was a problem because it was getting to the stage where places were so guaranteed your mother didn't ring to congratulate you any more.

The Irish hooker Rory Best knew what was going on and he came through to our dressing room and gave me his jersey and other Irish guys wished me well — my boots from that last test in Dublin are on my son Tyrell's wall. We managed to get him on the field and into the changing rooms and he's got some pretty cool photos with Kevvie and Richie, and we've got another of him earlier in the season, sitting inside the Bledisloe Cup.

I got off the plane and had a club T-shirt on because the kids had spilt stuff over the rest of my gear and that was it, happy days.

Getting through 2014 was easy. I was done and enjoyed life and footy for the club, but when 2015 rolled around I thought it would have been cool to be there. Now it's like: thank God I'm not playing that game any more where they get smashed up each week.

Rodney So'oialo was a good mate of mine at the Hurricanes and watching him hold on was not great. Instead of being remembered for the great player he was, he would come to training and try to get through it, and eventually I told him not to come to training because he was sucking it out of me.

I've always played for the Maniototo Maggots and had six games for them before the 2011 World Cup. It was much easier chasing the ball than running down the road and the coaches were fine about that. They worked out that a few of us liked a few beers and instead of saying no, they let us do our own thing.

It ticked us over.

Matt O'Connell played at the club and way before that Tony Kreft who drives for McLaren Transport. Tony Woodcock played for us when he was down here, and Hosea Gear, Tamati Ellison and James Haskell were all supposed to play but something happened. We struggle to get reserves, we have a 16-year-old and then there's me and the local policeman who is 42 and plays sometimes.

All Blacks physiotherapist Pete Gallagher drives up twice a week for our games and sorts out some surgeries and gives a great deal of his time and advice, so we rustle up some mutton to say thanks. I can't imagine the English physio driving out to the boondocks to give that sort of assistance.

She's good times but drinking and driving home — those days have gone now, and you don't want to put a teammate like the cop in an awkward position. The whole culture has changed. You used to go and help out your neighbour, then sit down and have a few beers and drive home, but you can't do that now.

There was nothing like the golden hour after footy. You can go and watch a game and have a beer with players, but that hour in the changing room, talking, taking your boots off and having a beer, even as a dirty-dirty it never felt the same because you hadn't actually been involved. I'd put myself on the bench for Maniototo and have 20 minutes to feel part of it and that's the best time, relaxing, having a few beers, a bit of banter about what happened.

I chatted on the field because that's my nature and it helped surviving with an older brother. Most of it was to get me relaxed and everyone has their ways of doing it. As you get older it gets easier and it was switch on and switch off. If I have a joke with you and you laugh then we're back into it. I think people can take life a bit too seriously at times.

When I first played for Otago we'd go into camp on Friday night before a Saturday game and people would stop talking then. Now you drive your car down an hour before kick-off. I think that mental side of the game has changed a huge amount — you don't have to walk around from Tuesday looking grim to prove you are focused.

Moving between the isolation on the farm to the crowds in town was great; if you got sick of one you'd do the other. Losing the 2007 World Cup was okay for me because I could concentrate on the farm and down at the club it doesn't matter if you played really good or bad. You'd go to training and they'd still give you shit.

I've never been good at watching, and I think the Super Rugby is shit and the Rugby Championship is the same. In my opinion, they make the mistake of adding more teams. I'm not sure I agreed with the Lions itinerary because I would have liked them to play the provinces and from their side of things, the midweek guys are not having a great time, which is what a tour should be all about. It was a cool tour, though, and it would be awesome to play them in a test series.

In future, I won't be on any boards or panels and if you are going to be a rugby coach you may as well be a player — it is full-time. Coaching the Maniototo boys is okay because we get by on the drills I learned 10 years ago.

Some people say I'm alright at speaking and some crowds are better than others and I'll do two or three a year like one Paul Tito arranged to celebrate the new facility in Taranaki before the test with Argentina. Rugby clubs are okay with Q&A sessions like the Waikaia rugby club's 125th celebrations when, as part of the deal, I flew in on a chopper, which took an hour instead of a four-hour drive.

At the Fieldays in Hamilton a year or so ago I think I enjoyed it too much and they did not ask me back. It feels weird getting paid to talk, but it's a good excuse or a good distraction like reunions where you have a few free beers and talk about how good you were.

Farming is a lot of family know-how and we don't get a lot of farm advisory stuff. When the old man wants to sell off sheep, for example, he just drafts them off at the gate — doesn't do figures. And when you shear the hoggets after you've drafted them off they'll always be between 16 and 18 microns. It's experience and that's why I wanted to go back to the farm before the old man was too old because while you grow up on a farm, it doesn't mean you are a farmer and because your old man is a doctor doesn't mean you know a lot about medicine.

You get ideas and there's nothing like getting with a few mates on a Sunday and having a few beers and driving around the farm discussing things. Frankie thinks we're nuts sitting in a truck drinking beer.

There's gold somewhere and one of Pete Gallagher's mates wants to grow arnica because there's a neighbour growing it. It's like an alpine plant that thrives in crap soil and they can use the worst bit of our farm.

We're not thinking about diversity. All my old man's money goes back into the farm, and he doesn't have a holiday house, but the good news is we don't have to put too much back into it at the moment. We are not going to try to make millions each year by changing things. One thing you learn in farming is the wheel always turns and we'll make the most of it when it's at the top, but if you are chasing it then the wheel turns again.

The old man has done a great job and on the whole farm I think there's probably only one gate that doesn't swing and he's got that measured up to get fixed. Machinery is expensive; we only have a set of discs and a grubber and a couple of tractors to feed out, that's all, and we get the contractors to do the rest. Tractors can cost up to a couple of hundred grand each. The old man can't start them, doesn't like them and he's never driven them, but he'll talk to you about sheep and cattle all day and night. He loves his horses, breaking them in and riding them, and I've inherited a bit of that and have a big guy who is laid back and goes to some good places but he's a bit 'unco'.

I'm going to wean myself off playing and into coaching because it's tough trying to get out of bed sometimes on Sunday and once you start playing your competitive gene kicks in.

Tyrell loves playing footy and that's great, while Esme wants to play hockey but she's only two.

Frankie and I met on a plane flying from Auckland to Wellington and she was sitting down, but if she had stood up I wouldn't have talked to her because she's a midget. I think she stalked me after that. I got her phone number and she showed up for Ma'a Nonu's 100th game for the Canes, then a week later I went to South Africa and she was still a 'livey' when I got home.

IAN JONES

Ian Jones represented New Zealand from 1989 to 1999, including in 79 tests, a record for a lock until 2016, and he scored nine test tries. He played for the Chiefs in Super Rugby and turned out for North Auckland and North Harbour. He later played in England for Gloucester Rugby and London Wasps.

Initially, after the 1999 World Cup, I went off on a two-year deal to England to play for Gloucester where a good friend of mine, the French captain Philippe Saint-André, was both player and coach. We were starting our family and it felt like a good place to go to work. The club was ambitious and owned by impressive businessman Tom Walkinshaw.

We lived in Cheltenham, which was a lovely part of England for my wife Janine and I to work and start our family.

For all of our relationship I was an All Black, and with the intensity of travel and playing, we were away a lot, but all of a sudden we were all there together in one house, 12 months of the year — one campaign, one club, one family. Wow. That was great for us and a total change.

Some of the rugby wasn't very good and it was a standard I could handle easily. There were some real characters at the club, World Cup winners Phil Vickery and Trevor Woodman and other internationals. It was a great time and a great fit.

I wanted to taper my rugby life rather than finish full stop. I wanted to spend time offshore with my family for the experience and we chose England because we had a new baby and the language made it easier than, say, going to Japan where we would have needed to make a lot more adjustments. The friendships and connections I made and learning about other perspectives in rugby ramped up tenfold. It was superb.

Without disrespecting any part of the New Zealand game, we only know the New Zealand way. That's what we're taught, what we understand, and we play really well. Going over to Europe expands that greatly and that's been shown with our coaches who go there like Wayne Smith, Steve Hansen and Graham Henry.

It expanded my rugby knowledge so much. I knew the New Zealand way inside out, about scrummaging and lineout drives, but to learn the Welsh way, and the English and French ways, gave me all these other pieces of the rugby pie. It was great to look at many different ways of solving the same problems.

I relished it. After another two years, though, we'd had another baby and around the end of 2001 some funny things started to happen.

I made two phone calls back to the New Zealand Rugby Union — and this is where it got really interesting. I distinctly remember I tried to talk to David Rutherford who was the chief executive. I got one of his deputies, introduced myself and told him I was playing in England and wondered what the chances were of doing something with NZR and their sponsors leading into the 2003 Rugby World Cup, assuming everything would have been in order or getting very close for that tournament.

I recall making the phone call and my wife remembers it well for them saying not everything is finalised yet with those contracts and we are still working through those details.

I hopped off the phone and said to Janine, 'Something is wrong there . . . the World Cup's not going ahead.'

I said if they haven't got things in place now it's not happening. Six months later it all fell over for New Zealand's co-hosting dreams.

What a mess. I assumed that they would have had major sponsors lined up from the UK, so I rang them again and spoke to someone in the commercial division. While things have changed now, I realised the NZR had no planning and no interest in their former players and their welfare.

I rang and told them I wanted to come back to New Zealand and wondered if there was anything there for someone like myself. I was asked what university degrees I had. I said I didn't have any because I had been playing for them for the last 11 years. Maybe now you can do a degree while you are an All Black, I don't know, but when we started we combined working with training and playing.

I was an apprentice electrician who became a tradesman in 1988 and an All Black the next year. I finished working when we came back from Wales at the end of that season because we were away so much. We got looked after before rugby went fully professional in 1995 but this was 2001, so being a sparky again was not on the horizon.

It floored me when I was asked about degrees or qualifications because I explained I'd been playing rugby for my employers.

Really, that just shut the door. In my opinion NZR didn't want any connection with former players and didn't want to do anything to help us. You were pretty much on your own coming back.

We came back in 2001 without any concrete plans. It was that sort of scenario and then about three weeks after being home, I got a call from Nigel Melville at Wasps who said the club needed a lock and asked me to go back and play.

I didn't have anything lined up in New Zealand. I'd been back to see the breweries and also Philips where I'd done some work for Errol McKenzie who was a wonderful man.

During my playing days, I transferred from North Auckland to North Harbour in 1994 and was employed at Lion Breweries then Lion Nathan to work alongside Iain Abercrombie and the All Blacks Club. We had wonderful sponsors with Philips, Ford, Telecom and Sky and at the end of 1995, the All Blacks Club had done what they could to get us to South Africa.

Alistair Sutherland, who was the chief executive of Philips NZ, asked me to come and work for them. They would put me through their departments and at the end of it there would be a job of my choice. That sounded brilliant.

At the end of 1995 rugby went pro and thankfully Philips was a big enough company to keep me on and help me through my career. As my rugby got busier they were very good to me and I still have an excellent relationship with them, Errol and Ian Marshall and others who were great mentors.

When we were back for those few weeks Errol offered me some of my old work, but we shot through to Wasps for another two years where Warren Gatland, Shaun Edwards and most of the Lions management were based.

Towards the end of our time there, I got a call from Graham

Veitch who was producing a TV programme called *GrassRoots Rugby* and had heard a whisper I was coming home and wondered if I could come and see him when I did.

I went back to work for Philips but also went to see Veitch and began working on his programmes in 2003 and I'm still doing it. From that hook-up he introduced me to Kevin Cameron at Sky and away I went — things snowballed from there.

I had no more desire to play competitive rugby, but there were a few charity games, coaching a tsunami benefit match in London with Rod Macqueen in 2004 and playing in another benefit game between Martin Johnson and Jonah Lomu's sides at Twickenham the year after.

I'm not a journalist but was experienced in rugby. While my hunger to play the game had dwindled, I was still really passionate about it. By the time I retired I'd had a great crack at it, I was proud of what I had done and loved all the opportunities that had been put in front of me. I was happy not to play but loved watching tests and I still buzzed about a game I did not need to play any more.

It was time. I was in my mid-thirties and hadn't had a break for 11 years, and funnily when you don't then play for a while you feel you could go on for another few years. But when we came home, I loved the idea of not having any schedules and not going to the gym or being at training and all those sorts of things. That's how it was for some months and at the end of that I didn't feel great, I was lacking energy and a few niggles you used to mask started to come back and haunt me.

So I got into adventure sport and triathlons and got fit again and haven't looked back. I had all these wonderful dreams about not having to train a great deal, but in reality I missed it and that's how I got back into it.

Getting fit for work at Sky was another issue.

I have been involved in rugby for a long time and never get sick of being around the game and the people. While I am not a trained broadcaster, I wanted to deliver my thoughts from the players' perspective and how they approached their work.

I knew how they were feeling during the week or when they ran out, how they would have to prepare or what they were doing when they assessed the opposition. That was how I went about my work thinking about the players' preparation.

For live television you have to be fully prepared and completely understand what you are talking about.

If you are passionate, others will feed off your passion, and working on the *GrassRoots* programme was a good stepping stone because we weren't in front of the camera.

Homework was key to working on live TV, understanding people, looking at players' strengths and weaknesses, and I still watch a lot of rugby. The more you do the better you refine what you do, and from the early days, I remember how Graham Henry and Wayne Smith had us watching stacks of videos, winding and rewinding, and now team analysts cut and clip segments for individual players.

I used to watch heaps of videos to find out things such as the fact that in two out of six lineouts in their 22, my opposition would throw to the middle, but now that information is given to the players. When Robin Brooke and I did our preparation, it wasn't nearly as refined, but it gave us a good idea that eight times out of 20 in one part of the field they were going to throw to the front.

In 2004 I worked through the provincial competition then Super Rugby and it helped being around the game a lot. You don't need a degree to know what you are talking about, but you have to connect it to whatever medium you are dealing with. You also have to be yourself and be true to your views.

My work coincided with a whole new era of coaches who were my contemporaries like Jamie Joseph, Mark Hammett and John Kirwan, guys I could always ring and feel comfortable talking to. That has always been easier than speculation and I still do that with Tony Brown, Tana Umaga, Steve Jackson or whoever is in charge.

Those guys are at the coal face every day and know I want to get an idea rather than divulge any secrets to their opposition or the public. I am trying to sell the game to give people a reason to watch it on Sky. Rugby watching has changed, especially in the quantity on offer, and you have to give people a reason to watch it. You mention the schools that players went to, the consequences of their work or how they compare; those sorts of insights help an audience.

At home I'll watch with my family and take note of something I'll want to go over later and can find very quickly on My Sky, which is a magnificent help. I work around my family needs and will get up early at 5 am or work late at night to sort out my Sky research.

That's never been an issue. My role changes all the time and this year I am doing analysis. I don't have to watch a lot of games to know what the strengths and weaknesses are in teams, but I need to think about how they will combat each other or take advantage of those areas.

I'm always thinking about the game and it might be on a bike ride or on a swim when I get my thinking time in doing those disciplines. I might be out on the bike for a two-hour cycle and I can think about what I am going to say. Sunday, Monday, Tuesday is Super Rugby then Wednesday recording

GrassRoots Rugby with Richard Mason and Graham Veitch.

The rest of my week is involved with mortgage broking. A good friend of mine, Norm Main, who had been in the game for a long time, offered to mentor me and that was too good an opportunity to turn down. I have been very busy. It's a long-term focus and I can still manage Sky, which also helps the profile.

I chat to families and get the best rates possible for whatever they need. It is about getting mortgages or reinvesting money with lending institutions; it is clean and focuses on people.

I understand the property game and every day I'm learning about this new direction. You have to work hard at it; you can't just open the door and expect things to happen. That never happened in sport and it won't in this either. It has fired me up to keep going in this direction, and I see it as a four- to five-year apprenticeship. Luckily, I am in a position to afford that time and you've always got to keep evolving.

I still get out on the speaking circuit and do some writing and have been mentoring sports journalism at school where they send their assignments to me and I critique them.

I love giving a few speeches and mingling and chatting with people; I manage all my gigs.

The busier the better. I like the phone ringing and helping people. I've been on the board at North Harbour Rugby, Rosmini College, Sport North Harbour, on the Shore to Shore committee and North Shore Swimming.

My fitness training continues to go well and I've done an ironman. You make the time. I have a big diary and we all have time we can use; if it's an hour at night, I'll go for a swim or a run. Life's good being busy, and it's all about managing your time.

One of the things about being an All Black is you are in a privileged position and rightly or wrongly it can open avenues; if you can use that to help people out, why not? I love the community where I live and if you give back, the response is so gratifying, you get so much more back. Being an All Black was great because it sets you up for all the values you live for today.

A lot of that is work ethic, as nothing comes easy. Being an All Black isn't easy and the guys who work the hardest get the better rewards. The more you put in the more you get out, and I still have a lot of time with my wife and three children.

The great thing I love about events is being with people who are there for the right reasons and the buzz is cool before and after when they have set their goals. The people and the communities I hang around with are also my social circles.

Some people might go to the pub on a Friday night for their relaxation and enjoyment while I will go for a ride in the Waitakeres or on Sunday go with former athletes and do a core session for a couple of hours and that is my social enjoyment. I still run, and there are plenty of places to go like a kayak mission to Rangitoto, a run up the top and then kayak back.

There is no way I'm as fit now as I was when I was an All Black. That meant everything to me, and playing a test match is harder than anything else I have done, harder than any ironman or GODZone adventure race, which are extreme events.

Nothing is as hard as representing your country for 80 minutes, not even close, mentally and physically. Representing the All Blacks, the amount of work you have to put in — nothing tops that. To me nothing compares to the fitness I had to have for that and nothing is as rewarding.

MICHAEL JONES

Michael Jones is acknowledged as one of the greats of All Blacks rugby. He played for Western Samoa in 1986 but debuted for the All Blacks the following year at the World Cup. He played in all three loose forward positions in a stellar career until 1998 that included 55 tests, scoring 13 test tries. In Super Rugby he played for the Blues, and he represented Auckland at provincial level.

I promised my wife when I retired I would burn my boots because I got injured enough when I was playing, so there was a high chance that if I tried to play a social match or a charity game I'd tear an Achilles tendon or blow my calf or pull a hamstring.

With such a long career and a tough journey through injuries, I was pretty clear in my mind that when I retired that was it, there would be no more. I wanted to pursue other things and I'd put that rugby part of my life behind me. I was very grateful for a full and long career, in years, and that I was able to enjoy some wonderful accomplishments and do lots of really cool stuff and I'd got that out of my system and I never pined for it afterwards.

I had done my dash in a good way. I was grateful but ready to get on with the next stage of my life.

Finishing with Auckland in the national championship was a beautiful thing while the accumulation of injuries made my last few years tough with the All Blacks.

Early in my career, I completed my studies in a seven-year block with a BA in economics and geography then town planning and then my Masters — I'd done that by 1990 and used that knowledge as an assistant lecturer at Massey University in 1991–92 when it had just opened. The work was flexible and quite concentrated because the students depended on you and occupied a decent part of my life alongside rugby.

Then I moved to Air New Zealand for a couple of years when Jim McRae was the boss, the cricketer Vaughan Brown was there and Anthony Mosse the swimmer — we were all in the same development section and I looked after the Pacific area, which linked with my studies on economic development and trade.

I only quit rugby when we had to sign full-time professional contracts, which meant little time for anything else. It was a time of transition in sport when we were not sure what was going to happen, but I put all my efforts into it. We had always been 'professional', so it felt unusual to then be full-time and well looked after for doing what we loved and enjoyed anyway, while I also worked hard with my family and the community doing voluntary work.

As my rugby career came to a close, it was time to rekindle ideas about life after that phase.

I was confident, excited and comfortable about it and wanted to sink my teeth into things I was passionate about because I had time to think about what it would look like.

Olo Brown and I worked on a project promoted by the government that was challenging and fun. It was sort of out of left field, but we thought it was an opportunity to do something positive for the Pacific community and provide us with a chance to dabble in business and the realities of the commercial world.

At that time, backyard butchery was a controversial subject, and we set up a wholesale and retail business and tried to provide a framework so Pacific Islanders did not have to go and buy home-kills and farm-gate kills.

We wanted to work with MAF and health and safety while providing options for purchasing a whole pig at a decent price. It was called Pacific Choice and it was fun. We were really hands-on and expanded into providing food like corned beef and chicken that Pacific communities need at funerals and weddings. We knew that space well because we had grown up in it and understood some of the inherent challenges.

It was about setting up a user-friendly model. We had a factory at Onehunga and a good line into the commercial world. Olo was the numbers man and I was into promotion and marketing and our aim was to eventually hand the business over to a community organisation. It was meant to be about an 18-month job alongside the government, but we stayed for about three years with MAF then it transitioned into a church trust to run.

Once that was sorted, I went to Auckland University of Technology where I was in management for seven to eight years driving the Pasifika strategy as the director of Pacific advancement inside the university and externally with the government and communities. It was the first programme of its type in New Zealand and there was a lot of engagement, developing and driving strategies from a very progressive university.

We pushed that work because traditionally Pacific Islanders at university were in pockets or little huddles; they weren't at the main table of decision making and were not engaged at the highest levels. We challenged that and really championed the cause in the early 2000s.

We got great support from people like Sir Toby Curtis who was the vice-chancellor of Maori development. A common theme for Pasifika is that we try to keep close to Maori because we have similar challenges, business statistics and education failure and were affectionately known as the 'long brown tail'.

It's something I have been passionate about coming from a family where education was very strong and my mother had been a secondary school teacher. We were always fighting to change the tail to the head or at least compress that tail in our lifetime.

We also believe we should be part of the head and not the tail. Education is a real key for Pasifika to move forward, and while sport has been a great way to position our people in this nation, education is the real key to move us from the tail.

That was the catalyst for us to organise a community trust where we worked with a lot of kids. Another Kelston old boy, Glenn Compain, and I set up a drop-in centre then began the Village in 1999. At the same time, we'd set up a trust to help kids out west and to assist their education and that has always been my passion, so the AUT thing was a nice transition. It allowed me to work full-time in tertiary education with the flexibility to work with our not-for-profit trust.

The Village is based on kaupapa and the idea that it takes a village to raise a child. I am a by-product of that because my dad passed away when I was four and my aunties and fathers did lots for me, and that is the kaupapa theme in West Auckland that underpins the Village Trust today. We have Friday-night drop-ins at Kelston College and mentoring at schools, sports academies and now under another trust, in South Auckland, the Pacific Advance Senior School (PASS), which has been going for several years.

It's tough going, almost like a last resort for kids who have been kicked out of school at, say, 15 but whose numeracy and literacy might be only that of a 10- or 12-year-old and their behaviour patterns, mindsets and habits are ingrained.

Alongside that new work, I worked with John Boe coaching Samoa, which was all about my love of rugby and my nation, and when John retired they asked me to be head coach, so I tried to balance that in my schedule. There was no money in Samoan rugby and working at AUT put pressure on them there, so I took a job in the commercial world in 2007, in shipping, working for Matson.

It was time for a change and I designed my work in the commercial world in the Pacific to fit alongside my coaching. I was based in Auckland and had to travel a lot to Samoa and proposed a model they have adopted now for a full-time coach to help player development.

Working for Matson has been about strategic development. We have a general manager and I spend about 60 per cent of my time working on economic and social fusion in the Pacific and the rest of my time is spent in the community.

We have a bulk fuels division that supplies ships from Fiji, Samoa, Niue, Tokelau, the Cook Islands, Samoa, American

Samoa and Tonga including Vava'u as well as managing the relationships between government, business and community. It's quite a network. We source our fuel from New Zealand and use 20-foot isotainers to carry diesel, petrol, jet fuel and LPG. We are a lifeline for the islands and the job is a wonderful privilege with a lot of responsibility. The supply has to be cost effective and punctual because we will hear about it if the food, alcohol and fuel does not arrive on time.

That job keeps my connections to the Pacific strong and my community work, which is my real passion, is also working well. It is a vocation and will be with me forever.

I've never wanted to leave Auckland because as Pacific Island/Kiwi/Samoan people we need to grow our leadership through the next generations and into the next levels of decision making, whether it is corporate, government or not-for-profit areas. My work is here, home is here, and this is my community.

We have good people but not enough leadership. We have a sense of responsibility to reinvest in the communities that shaped us. I am more value to my communities and can effect more transformation in the roles I'm doing and create change by working at the grassroots rather than being on a council or running for mayor because that is a different model. I've never felt like getting into politics; I believe in working with these people from the bottom up.

We have strong relationships with central government and other bodies, but my personal gift that rugby gave me as an All Black is a platform to influence and effect change from the grassroots. I can move more freely without having a political agenda and I think I can achieve more, help more and challenge from this space.

I sit on the Whanau Ora board for Pasifika because it is an

effective programme and 99 per cent of the boards I sit on get some sort of funding. You have to be strategic and while rugby has given me a great platform, you have to be a really good steward of that influence and your time and that is my challenge.

Things don't just happen, but when I'm driving in my car I have space to think, I have coffee with good people, I wake up in the night strategising and thinking how we can do things better, how we fill this gap, where we get funding, and what are the practical steps we have to take.

The waka is driving those targets and 90 per cent of my focus is West Auckland, South Auckland and programmes involving Pacific people in general. The Village and the Pacific Peoples Advancement Trust are two key boards I chair.

I've got to say no a bit more because my family is growing up fast. However, I think we have got a good balance with family, work and service. Maliena and I got married in 1994 and we have a daughter Tiara who is 18 and at university, Niko is 16 and goes to St Peter's and my youngest Levi is six and we also have two foster kids, 10 and 12. I protect that home environment and if I can't get that right I have failed because I don't want them to suffer because I am out trying to save the world type of thing.

Nights and weekends are family time, but there is a lot of dovetailing, a lot of invitations and priorities.

I was president of Waitemata Rugby Club for four years but have stepped down because I have done my time and coached and that's important too. I don't get down there as much because Niko plays at the same time, but it's a good club and I've got a lot to be thankful to them for, for being part of my life and part of my village.

Church is my way of life and we are part of the Community

Christian Fellowship, which is an independent evangelical interdenominational movement who meet on Sundays in Kelston. Our congregation is led by my brother and his wife who are our pastors, and my wife and I are part of that leadership.

When the missionaries arrived in the Pacific Islands with their religion it was like having a light switched on. One of my great-great-grandfathers is buried in Vanuatu and was one of the first Samoan missionaries after John Williams introduced the Gospel throughout the Pacific. It is our heritage, gives us a moral compass and a sense of purpose and it underpins our values.

By now I thought I would have needed a new right knee, but I have talked to my surgeon Stu Walsh who says as long as I am mobile and jog for half an hour most mornings on the treadmill that's fine. If I don't exercise it will seize up, so it's my version of use it or lose it. Walking is not as comfortable because of the scar tissue, but I only sleep four or five hours a night, so I can jog and use light weights in the garage before I leave for work because I won't do it when I get home.

My left knee and the patella tendon injury is stable, my shoulders are fine and I'm a little arthritic, although I don't take anti-inflammatories and am not yet like a lot of my old mates who have new hips and knees. Strangely, the only bone I broke was my jaw in 1993.

What will the future look like in 10 years? I'll be in Auckland; I'll never leave the west. I have mulled over things and I'm not sure how long I'll stay in the shipping business, but if anything, I'll be more involved in the communities with some special-interest projects.

I'll be on some boards because that is the changing face of contemporary Aotearoa and where I can achieve a great deal. I spoke to Sir Wilson Whineray many times and he was a great man who helped at Dilworth and was on some powerful boards and struck a balance with community work he was passionate about. I might return to more education work, but my hands-on work will be west and south, driving the waka, leading Pasifika.

It will be about building a team and getting people to come with me and getting great lieutenants. If we don't drive them, reading the stars and feeling the wind, it won't happen. It is a mission, and we are missionaries for change; it is evangelical. We have targets and want to catch up because we are so far behind and need to get going.

Lack of hope or ambition and a sense of hopelessness is the tough part — we want to be a circuit-breaker for those intergenerational habits. We see the symptoms, crime and lawlessness, but we want to work on people's potential and steer them towards a stronger life. Sometimes it's too late because working with wet cement is okay but not concrete, so it's better to invest in areas where you can make a difference, working smart and being savvy.

It is not about hui-huis, it is about doi-dois on our part.

I think of my mother, a young widow from the Islands who did some amazing things and was forever the optimist. Her attitude was so remarkable — we had to keep moving, forget about the mire — and I think I have inherited that and it re-energises me.

JOSH KRONFELD

Josh Kronfeld debuted as flanker in 1995 and was a key All Black until 2000, with 54 tests and 14 test tries. He played for the Highlanders in Super Rugby and represented Otago. He went on to play for English club Leicester Tigers.

Once I played my last test, I thought I'd stay in New Zealand. If things started to get a bit stale, challenges would come from new kids on the block like Ron Cribb, Troy Flavell, Norm Maxwell and Scott Robertson and that reinvigorated me.

There was also a transition in the way the game was played as we had got pretty obsessed with the superstar player, the single player, the Jonah Lomu syndrome if you will — because that's probably where it started.

There were individuals who weren't really team men in terms of playing. I'm not talking the social aspects here, I'm talking about guys who would try to make a play when they had teammates alongside them. That's what made them great players and I don't begrudge that because some of them in that era were the greatest attacking players I've ever seen in my life.

But coming from the Otago mentality and my role there and the way that evolved, it was all about link and team and support and keeping the play rolling, and if you can't score the try you are thinking I'll shift it to someone who can give it back to you to score.

So I was getting a little despondent with All Blacks rugby to a point, because you'd chase someone yelling, 'I'm here, I'm here,' and they'd end up dying with the ball.

I felt like I was becoming a stats man, first to the ball, high-level numbers for cleanout, turnover ball, tackle numbers — love those things because they were my game — but I liked running with the ball. Maybe I wasn't as fast as I had been but pretty close, and that's how I felt, and it was getting me down a bit.

The New Zealand union wasn't expressing any interest, although they said they wanted to keep me but couldn't afford to at my previous salary. Imagine them saying that to Richie McCaw, not that I'm putting myself in his category, but I felt affronted by that.

I blew it, I think. If I had another go at it, I wouldn't have mentioned I was leaving at the end of the year. When I said that, they treated me differently, and I should have just finished out 2000 and gone. After I signed to leave New Zealand and the All Blacks had toured Japan, France and Italy, the coaches said they would have taken me on to keep me at home, while the union offered me a mad-dash contract. I'd signed by then and was a man of my word, so I went to Leicester, which was the worst signing in the world.

They had a really good incumbent with Neil Back and another young guy, Lewis Moody, so I figured I wouldn't get smashed about too much and then whoever was good enough come playoffs time would get the work. But I only played one quarter-final in my time there when the club went to all the big playoffs. All I did was sit on the bench.

Leading up to the quarter-final in my second year when we lost against Munster at home, I'd been player of the match about four or five times in a row and they gave me player of the month for the Heineken Cup on the Wednesday and interviewed me on TV. The next day I was dropped to the bench. Dean Richards and John Wells were coaching us and I went in and swore at them and asked what I'd done wrong and tried to get them to justify their selections.

They couldn't, and I told them they were treating me as an extra. I went on with about 15 minutes left and scored two tries and set up a third. I didn't have a great rapport with those coaches.

Leicester was way too central for me, not coastal, but when you looked on the map you are thinking like a Kiwi and that it'd be really easy to get places, but it's not. Everything took a long time and everything I did in the UK was the wrong decision.

At the start of that second season, Leicester asked me to look for a new club because I wasn't getting many minutes and then something turned up on the news reporting that I wasn't happy and was looking for a new club. Then they had injuries to both openside flankers and it was 'Hey buddy, come on down.'

In 2003, Back and Moody were going to the World Cup, so Leicester wanted to keep me for half a season to cover for them being in camp with England. I even captained the club in a few games, but it wasn't hard to leave.

I went travelling for about 10 months from 2003 into 2004, going through the Americas. I hired a Harley-Davidson and had a fantastic time motoring around living in a tent. The USA is massive but I didn't realise quite how big. You unfurl the map and aim for some place that looks a good ride and it turns into 12 hours of concentration. I did about 15,500 miles on the Harley and while I didn't have my surfboards I stayed at a few places where I could borrow some and get into it.

Once I got the bike sorted, I got on the road to LA then San Francisco and Oregon and across Washington and down through Montana and back to Arizona and buzzed across to Texas, New Mexico and into the Grand Canyon, across to LA again then headed for Mexico.

After a while I flew to Chile, bought a truck and was meant to go to Argentina and Patagonia and north to Peru, but every time I took my vehicle in they thought I had stolen it. I got arrested maybe three times for stealing my own car. However, I had a letter which proved my ownership, but every time they'd ring about that, it would take time before it was verified. While frustrating, it wasn't nerve-wracking, although I joined up with people at different times, making it more sociable.

Chile was like I imagine New Zealand was 90 years ago, still pretty rugged with people living off the land. They were sociable, giving, accepting people and, unlike Peru, you couldn't bribe their police. I got adopted for three weeks by a family I'd made contact with through the International Rugby Academy of New Zealand and I did some coaching while I was there. The week I arrived was Chile's national day, so that was a party for a week before I went surfing in some of their great spots.

Then it was down to Patagonia, catching ferries as far as you could go south then across to Argentina where I was worried about getting back with the car, so I had a month in Peru — where my passport was stolen. I couldn't get to Ecuador then the Galapagos because of the passport issue, so I flew back through Easter Island then to New Zealand after almost a year on the road.

Getty

Hard work but another All Blacks triumph against England in 2007 when Frank Bunce beats Chris Sheasby at the Bob and Weave celebrity boxing ball in Old Billingsgate.

NZ Police

Glen Osborne carries the pride of his family and his grandfather's korowai at his police graduation.

Getty

Sean Fitzpatrick delivers the message as chairman of the Laureus Academy during a 2016 summit in Germany.

Getty
Getty

They experienced the gamut of opinions about their time as All Blacks, now
Mark Allen, Matthew Cooper, Andrew Mehrtens and Justin Marshall are
broadcasting their thoughts.

Getty

Getty

Christian Cullen and Jeff Wilson, who played 41 tests together, have teamed up again to give their televised views on the national game.

Getty

Getty

Not many players take on coaching, but Blair Larsen, Craig Dowd and Walter Little all took up that challenge.

Getty

Getty

Getty

Getty

Former All Blacks manager John Sturgeon presents caps to Richard Loe, Arran Pene and Adrian Cashmore.

Getty

Outstanding All Blacks flanker Michael Jones is inducted into the
International Rugby Hall of Fame in 2003.

Getty

Norm Hewitt and MP Paula Bennett launch a nationwide plan to tackle children's social, education and health issues in 2011 in Auckland.

Getty

All Blacks captain Kieran Read and his daughters listen as Keven Mealamu presents the No. 8 with his 100th cap after the drawn third test and series against the Lions at Eden Park, 2017.

Warren Buckland/Hawke's Bay Today

Fishing interests from Hawke's Bay down to Te Anau are part of Taine Randell's wide-ranging business portfolio.

Getty

Competitive instincts continued for John Timu as he suited up for the 2003 Speight's Coast to Coast race.

Getty

Josh Kronfeld showed off his moves with *Dancing with the Stars* partner
Rachel Burstein before a Super Rugby game in Dunedin in 2009.

Getty

There's no mistaking the loping stride and grit from Ian Jones as he competes in the Port of Tauranga Half Ironman in 2009.

Stuff/Fairfax NZ

The New World for Eric Rush is running a supermarket franchise, this one in Kaikohe.

Natalie Campbell/Hereford Prime

Beer and banter at a Hereford stud at Roxburgh in 2013 as Andrew Hore and Tony Woodcock got through their routines.

Rugby was out of my system by then, although I wouldn't mind playing the modern game with all the action, but I get frustrated at the way they dilute the contact; I can't understand that. Rules about head-high tackles have got a bit lame, although I applaud ideas about reducing concussion.

While I'd been away I enrolled in university to do a physiotherapy degree. Initially, I wanted to do osteopathy, but when I applied for the school they wouldn't let me use my phys-ed degree, so I enrolled in physio, which allowed me some of those credits.

It was still a three-year degree. I was living on my student allowance with a few jobs here and there and my rugby earnings.

Then all those television programmes like *Treasure Island* started cropping up and when Julie Christie said she wanted me to appear I just laughed. Somehow we did the deal and the first season of *Treasure Island*, which I won, was the most hilarious and one where I forged some great friendships. After the day's business, we'd light a bonfire with guys like Maz Quinn and Simon Barnett and sit around shooting the breeze and the girls from the other camp would come over and join us: Charlotte Dawson, Aja Rock and Lana Coc-Kroft — who had to be evacuated out.

One night we talked religion for about three hours and the next day might have been the flipside like the sex industry; you had nothing else to do except converse.

On the second *Treasure Island* series, the dynamics changed completely because all the prize money went to the winner. It was nothing like the first season. There was bitching and carping and editing the footage, and I swore I'd never do another even though we were paid to be there. I won the prize money and gave a significant amount to my Koru Care charity.

With the rest of the money I went to buy a motor scooter, but the boys at McIver & Veitch, the motorcycles company in Dunedin, talked me into buying a Motard so I went from a $3000 buy to a $17,000 purchase.

There was also a spell working on breakfast TV with April Ieremia where I was totally out of my comfort zone, although at the end they were happy with the dynamic between us. April was next level, great to work with but demanding.

Once I qualified as a physio, I worked in several practices with some locum work in Dunedin and then filling in with similar situations up north. Things were also starting to tick over with Sky too with a mini-rugby show, so I had a great mix of work.

It was all about finding out where I sat because my television role was not defined. Being with the *Crowd Goes Wild* show feels more comfortable now, although at times I feel like we go more for the gag than we do for the news, but lots of people love that.

Around the tail end of my university career I met Bronwyn and then did long-distance romance for a year or so before settling with her in Auckland. We have two boys. Cassius had a difficult birth and has a manageable degree of cerebral palsy and is seven and realising his limitations. That creates a new dynamic because he is very spirited. Arlo is four and a good little man.

Bronwyn went back to work pretty much straight away each time and I have been a house dad, which has changed my thought patterns from being free to do whatever and whenever I wanted, to looking after the boys. I involved both boys in whatever I was doing, whether it was working at *Crowd* or at a rugby seminar or at lunches. They're a great group to work with and I've increased my skills in presenting, developing stories, editing and filming, which I've done a few times. I don't mind making a fool of myself for the sake of the story and usually leave it to the technicians to put it together.

I also work three nights a week doing physio, but that reduces in the rugby season when I like to coach and that takes priority. I've worked as a technical advisor at Suburbs with all age groups and that takes up as much time as I can give them. I also did some work at Eden at the Colts level where I tried to give them some ideas beyond the handouts from rugby development officers.

I want to upskill players and the coaches as well, and I love the whole science behind it. I think if I was going to do next-level development I would have to revisit some courses. Having said that, as much as rugby has moved on, it hasn't changed that much. There are technical nuances and specific drills, but they are all versions of an older template.

Half the reason I have kept in touch with rugby and communicating is because I may do that in the future, but it is an all-in thing and I don't have the time right now. You speak to Wayne Smith or Steve Hansen and they'll tell you about the huge pressures on your home life because you are really adopting another family. At the moment, Bron's business is a key part of what she is focused on and one of us has to be around the kids and cover the home needs.

My interest in physio is in the solution, the treatment side of things. Sometimes when I'm working I've had enough of the talk and that empathy thing can get awkward because you are dealing with people all the time. Life is constantly about juggling time, using the diary on the computer and making sure I keep that up to date.

I still mess it up and missed an appointment the other day.

The beach, the surf, the music — they've all been me. Surfing happens once or twice every few weeks. It runs in binges, but I miss a lot of good waves these days and the body hurts more than it used to. If I was surfing every day or twice a week it would be great, but I don't get in the water enough. My favourite break on the west coast is probably out by Port Waikato because it's isolated and rugged, or at Piha, and if you're on that regularly, then you get in tune with it. The only difference between here and down south is there are going to be a lot more people in the water with you.

The music has gone. I've got all the instruments sitting there and the boys play around with them and jump on them, and if I bump into Midge Marsden he asks me to get on the stage but I can't; I'm too embarrassed because I don't play enough. I hear music easily, but I can hear how much I am off and I don't like it. It's like anything: it's motor programming, muscle memory and once you tune muscle memory to the rhythm of music you are in the link, you can go anywhere and then it's just a matter of reprogramming that memory for a new note or tweak or chord.

Our place down at Raglan is still there and as awesome as it was 20 years ago, but we can't go there on a whim now because it's rented out. We get there every third year for about a month and then we'll go for a fortnight somewhere around Christmas and will do 10 days or so in Wanaka and then Hawke's Bay.

BLAIR LARSEN

Blair Larsen was first chosen for the All Blacks as a lock in 1992 but spent most of the rest of his career, until 1996, at flanker. He appeared in 17 tests and scored one test try. He played for the Chiefs in Super Rugby and represented North Harbour and Northland. He later played for Kobe Steel in Japan.

I began my working life in the police force without any real idea about the future and now I'm working for The Drug Detection Agency, a company which caters for safer workplaces and offers solutions for all drug policy, education and testing needs.

We started a dozen years ago to deliver a customised service to companies who want to conduct drug and alcohol testing within their organisations. As part of my portfolio, I'm in charge of growing the business in Australia and helping companies with ideas around on-site drug-detection strategies.

Our founder and chief executive is Kirk Hardy who was with the New Zealand Police drug squad targeting drug syndicates and organised criminal groups before he set up TDDA as an on-site testing and education service and then, in 2011, established TDDA in Australia.

We employ top scientists, and companies love using us as a tool to steer people into better habits and make their environments safer. I talk to companies about what we do and how we can help them. We are not a law enforcement agency, but we can help companies with safe work practices and they can decide what they do with the results.

It's been more than 20 years since my last All Blacks test as a sub for Ian Jones in that series win against South Africa in 1996 and 15 years since my last game of footy. I swim a bit these days to try to keep weight off.

I wasn't going to leave New Zealand until I'd done all I could and my time in the All Blacks had come to an end. Then it was a natural progression to shift to Japan where the game had gone professional, you could make a good living and it was a cool chance to take my wife Jackie away for a different hit at life.

Before I signed, I went up there with Joe Stanley, who was my agent, and had a look around and Kobe Steel seemed a great fit. I was incredibly lucky to end up with the team I did. It's very much luck of the draw when you go around and see where some of the other players end up.

I spent four seasons working for Kobe, about an hour's drive south of Osaka, which is the nicest metropolitan area in the country. Taking the World Cup to Japan in 2019 will be such a superb experience with the people, the language and the whole flavour of the country.

We were the Auckland of Japan rugby with half the national side, and for the first few years we won every game. It was fun. Our mega star was Andy Miller, who was the equivalent of

Jonah Lomu in New Zealand, but few knew him back here from his time with Canterbury, the Crusaders and in sevens. He'd been with Kobe for a couple of years before I arrived and kicked all the goals and ran in stacks of tries and was the headline act in most matches.

Another Harbour man, Richard Turner, played for another team nearby and we were big guys there, but that didn't count for much because when you tried to run over your rivals, they cut you off around your ankles, so you had to learn to evade and run around defenders. The rugby wasn't as physical as we were used to and I liked that change of style.

Their philosophy, though, was quantity over quality and it was about doing more rather than — and I don't want to be disrespectful here — necessarily doing it better. Sometimes we would train for three hours in 30-degree heat in summer and that was a sporting and cultural difference.

My eldest son Bronson was born up there and eventually was a big part of the reason for coming home. He developed viral meningitis and it was quite scary how it panned out because he was initially misdiagnosed before someone from our apartment building, a paediatrician, insisted we should take him for further testing. He ended up in hospital because meningitis heats your brain and affects your motor skills, and it took him a while to get over it. There is a little bit of a hangover from that illness to this day, but we were lucky.

In my fourth season, Jackie was heavily pregnant with our second boy, Duke, and we decided it was not the place for a young child to be. She came home just before I finished up and when I got back to New Zealand she was about to give birth.

Living in Japan was a fantastic introduction to another culture and learning another language, which I probably didn't get to grips with as much as I should have but enough to converse. It was a great time, a great experience, the lifestyle was brilliant and the people too and they made us feel very welcome. We travelled to Thailand and Malaysia and it was so close to lots of great places, whereas in New Zealand unless you can go to the Pacific islands or Australia every other trip is long haul.

When we came back I pulled on the Harbour jersey again in 2003 and that was a big mistake. It was a mix of nostalgia with Allan Pollock as the coach and being a bit selfish because I was close to 100 games and I liked the idea of having one last run around, but it was the wrong thing to do. It was hard yakka playing with all these young guys who were so fit. I had some serious back issues and I shouldn't have attempted it, but I did and that was it.

When I finished with footy I was thinking about another career but was uncertain. That's where I think players these days get much better support because you are taught to think about having a plan in place, whether it be tertiary education or networking to find something you want to be in or running your own business.

I don't think players reached out as much at that time and I certainly didn't. I wasn't a great networker then and that's a key thing. Certainly, the advice I pass on to any young rugby player is that you have the best environment in which to network and you never know when that is going to come in handy.

You are always at after-match functions or sponsors' meetings and you need to be the person putting your hand up to ask how you can be involved. There are so many opportunities, but when you are a young player you don't realise that and you are selfish and restricted in your vision outside the game.

My advice to young guys would be network while you can and, while you are doing that, find out what you might end up doing once the rugby days are done. If you don't have some form of qualification, there are a million you can get through the tertiary providers. It doesn't have to be a BCom; you can be a greenkeeper or a beekeeper and playing rugby will pay for it.

I'd been looking for a business and ended up buying a milk round delivering for Anchor. They do psychometric testing to work out if you are the correct candidate for their brand. Quite a few players were getting into that line of work and you hear about it and investigate and I sat in a truck, did my diligence, learned from the owner and had a franchise for about three years. I bought an existing run that covered quite a large area around Silverdale.

My next idea was to do some coaching, so I went to Sicily in 2007 and worked for the Amatori Catania club, but that only lasted a short time before family reasons brought me back home. I was keen to stay around home and coach Harbour but missed out on that and got a job as Northland assistant to Bryce Woodward in 2008.

I found I needed to be more connected with my kids back in Auckland so bought into the Pita Pit franchise with a store in the Britomart complex. That was a hands-on business with about 10 other staff. It wasn't really me, however, so I moved on and renovated a house we owned while I thought about something else.

Rugby coaching or being involved in the sport was still in the front of my mind and I was close to working in Australia on a project but eventually it didn't happen.

Along the way I met a new partner, Sally, who has a boy and girl, and we have been engaged for about four years and it's a bit like the Brady bunch, doing all the things you have to do with Bronson doing well in water polo — that's his big thing — while Duke is still into footy.

Then this job came up at TDDA where I'll talk to companies about what we do and how we can help them. We have about 40 branches across New Zealand and one of my old rugby rivals, Errol Brain, heads up one of our workplaces in Tauranga.

Sally and I have got a place up on the coast at Omaha where I love to go out in my 6.5-metre tinny. I'll go fishing for anything, as it's so relaxing out on the water, but the success rate means the fish we catch are probably twice as expensive as buying them. But it's a great way to while away a few hours, and having that family time is so important.

WALTER LITTLE

Walter Little spent most of his All Blacks career, 1989–98, as second five-eighth, including in a celebrated midfield pairing with Frank Bunce (see earlier in this book). In his 50 tests he scored nine tries. He turned out for the Blues in Super Rugby and represented North Harbour. He also played for Sanyo club in Japan.

After my days with the All Blacks I played a few more seasons of Super Rugby and then moved to Japan. I loved it there and wish I'd gone earlier. Everything about it was great: the culture, the food, the rugby and all the people in the sport and outside it. They were so kind and courteous and there was little crime over there that we heard about.

Now my eldest son Michael is playing over there. It was a shame he did not get a Super Rugby contract here. I think the Highlanders were keen on keeping him, but it was too late then because he'd signed for two years with a Japanese club.

I played for Sanyo and our coach was Murray Henderson, an ex-army guy from down Canterbury way and very strict. I had to manage myself fairly well over there because the Japanese play their rugby from side to side with very good skills and fitness. We also had Greg Coffey in the team and Mike Cron was doing some of our coaching to help out. They were a good crew and in my two and a half years up there they tried to get us to play a bit like Canterbury of course.

In the end you know when you have run out of gas and the old injuries are taking longer to come right. I had a slight neck injury as well as my knee problem, so I thought it would be better to come home.

I didn't really know what I wanted to do once my career in New Zealand wound down with a couple of seasons for North Harbour and the Blues. I spoke to people in real estate, but I wasn't sure about that and still had a bit more time up my sleeve.

Offers of overseas contracts were coming through all the time, but I left all that to Bruce Sharrock who I played against and was starting to get into work as a player agent.

Coaching overseas didn't interest me, and I was happy just to play. That's why I had decided it was best to take the family away and live in Japan, learn about all the things in life there and play some rugby. Tracey and I had three kids then — we've got five now — and we just wanted to get out of New Zealand for a while. Michael is the oldest at 23, then Daniel, Josh, Christopher and Ali — who is the youngest and our only daughter.

It was awesome having all our kids with us. We had the option of throwing them into an international school, which was a bit away from where we were staying, or putting them into a Japanese school. We went with the Japanese school and within two weeks they were speaking the language; they just soaked it up.

We had Japanese lessons. I wasn't too bad and can still understand it if people speak slowly and can still read it and speak enough to order my food and grog. If Tracey was going shopping, she would take the kids with her and they would do a lot of the translating.

We all loved it at Gunma Prefecture, about an hour's drive north-west of Tokyo. When you talk to the Japanese boys they believe it's too far out in the country and there's nothing there, but we loved it and so did lots of Brazilians who live there.

When it came time to think about a job back in New Zealand, I wasn't sure what would happen. My elder brother Charlie was doing contract scaffolding, so after a fortnight at home — we'd bought a couple of apartments so that was bringing in some money — I wanted to get out and work, so I started with him.

He gave me a solid grounding in the work. He'd been in the game for about 20 years and I loved it. Everything suited me, from getting up early in the mornings, being outdoors in the fresh air to the manual work rather than sitting behind a desk. It helped keep me reasonably fit for a bit of playing and coaching.

After a while I got sick of working for someone else and started Little Scaffolding Ltd, and my brother came and worked for me. He was contracting and put the idea into my head about starting up my own company and I was keen to do that.

I needed to set up the business, get the tickets and my papers as an advanced scaffolder, which I did in 2005 at Tai Poutini Polytechnic in Onehunga in a year when you work around your study blocks. That helped with the technical details around the infrequent work like cantilevers or accessing difficult ground. Your maths has to be good to work out the fulcrum points and counterweights and safety requirements because if you don't know how to do it you don't take on the difficult work.

We undertake the lot, and a great deal of residential work can be quite technical where we use the tube and clip system because you can do anything with it and it is very solid. If you use a modular system, it can be a bit harder.

When we were looking around for a depot we came across a placc in Silverdale that seemed a long way out of town, but when we looked at it, the factory seemed perfect and it wasn't far from home.

In those days my brother and I got work by cold-calling sites and asking builders and leaving our cards, advertising and flyers. Now people come to us because it's all word of mouth or from seeing our signs on the toe boards. Builders, small housing companies and clients like to line us up for work.

We try to do a house a day. In good weather, two men can put up about 250 square metres in a day for a standard house, and if we do five houses a week with one truck that's great, while I've got another out the back which needs a new gearbox.

For the first two or three years, I was answering the phone, measuring up, doing quotes, putting up the scaffold then doing invoices until midnight, but it had to be done if I wanted my business to be successful and rugby had drilled that sort of discipline into me. As we got busier we asked around for a few more staff and I got off the tools.

We have not had any accidents or had tubes or fittings drop, just the odd broken window but nothing major. Safety is number one for us and we always ask our guys at the end of the job if they would be happy working on the scaffolding they have put up.

It's very much about keeping the clients happy. The hours

vary depending on how far we travel and how hard the work has been. We try to keep the weekends free because our bodies are tired by then.

I enjoy it, I'm not in the office too much and go to job sites where you meet a lot of good people from all walks of life, including a few old rugby contacts like Ben Afeaki who was in looking at what we did because he was thinking about doing something similar.

Not long after we returned from Japan, Russell Jones phoned wanting me to come back and play for Harbour again. I told him I was 33 and that was it, I'd had enough of the rep stuff, but I did play a few games for my Glenfield club, although training on cold nights after work was a bit much.

I got by. At that age I'd learned a few tricks and it wasn't hard. I didn't want to play any more provincial stuff though. I'd lost interest in that but was happy going back to grassroots, and giving back to the game was something I was interested in. That's why I ended up coaching at Glenfield and got the job with the premiers, probably because of who I was and the fact I knew more than a lot of others at the club.

We had guys like Mark Hellyer who rang and asked for help. The club was still young and rebuilding, but in three years we ended up getting Glenfield to a final. It was a good opportunity for me to learn a lot about the scene and the rugby was a good standard.

I love coaching. The more it went on I thought about taking some of the coaching courses — that's what you have to do now if you want to go any further up the ladder in your career. Otherwise you are fine. I talked to people at Harbour about it and how I'd had some experience with the provincial age-group sides and they offered to help me with the courses, but I haven't got around to doing it because of work, family and coaching at Glenfield.

I was curious about coaching at provincial level and helped Steve Jackson when he was at Harbour, which was an eye-opener in terms of what they do these days at the semi-professional level. However, running this scaffolding business then coaching around that doesn't quite work.

Coaching Glenfield this year got a miss too. They weren't doing very well and their backs coach asked me if I could come and help, but I wanted to take time out to help my boy Christopher, who has only played for a few years at Massey High School where he's a loosie or second-five, before I decide whether I want to have another crack next year. I've coached on and off for about eight years and love it and will do some more but probably only at club level.

I'm big on basic skills, ball work and handling because a lot of the game is played in your head. I try to give players a pattern and then it's all about vision, asking them to look at what's in front of them and making decisions from there. If it's on to have a go, do it, and the support players have to understand what can happen and need to be switched on. It's really about open play and looking at what's on around the paddock. It just needs everybody to be alert and on a similar wavelength.

Club rugby players tend to dream a lot. Even if they are on the wing they stand around looking at the crowd and not concentrating on what's happening. A lot of coaching is getting players to focus on skills, footwork and being smart about how you are going to play.

It is frustrating at times, but I'm big on talking to players after training and seeing how they felt in certain situations and asking them to talk about how they saw a game and getting their feedback.

I don't want to be the one talking to the players all the time; I don't want to dictate. I want them to tell *me* why they did certain things. Getting them to think is half the battle, as you win more games using your brain than you do with brawn. There are some really good kids out there, but it is a matter of channelling them, giving them a focus and goals and targets, and telling the team we'll only reach those goals if we all have similar ideas.

The majority of club players turn up fit, but it's the props and big boys who take a bit more work because it's hard on their joints. They don't like training or the hard fields and the last couple of years I kept them off the track with boxing and alternative trainings to hold their interest and get them fit.

At Glenfield, our only other All Black was Mark Mayerhofler, who was also a midfield back. We've had other internationals, my brother Lawrence, who has a scaffolding company out Botany way, my nephew Nicky, and Issy Tuivai who played for Tonga and Frances Latu who played for Tonga at halfback.

I watch as much footy as I can and I go to a few reunions. We had a great one during the Lions tour getting together with Arthur Stone, Vic Simpson and Frano Botica, and the last trip I went on was a Legends tour to South Africa about eight years ago with Bill Bush and Jock Ross. We were supposed to get through about five games in a week, but that was a bit much for all of us.

It showed me I should stick to family, watching footy and scaffolding.

RICHARD LOE

Prop Richard Loe was part of a dominant All Blacks front row that also featured Sean Fitzpatrick (see earlier in this book). He represented New Zealand from 1986 to 1992 and 1994–95, including 49 tests, and scored six test tries. He played for the Crusaders and the Chiefs in Super Rugby and represented Canterbury, Marlborough and Waikato.

If it hadn't been for Laurie Mains I'd have stopped playing before the 1995 World Cup, but he wanted a third prop he could trust because the next guy was a bald-headed vegetarian from Taranaki who went to the Turbos and I don't think that fitted Laurie's ideas.

I could do all the work he wanted and being on that trip led to a whole lot of interesting conversations from which professional rugby developed in this country. If it wasn't for the New Zealand Rugby Union coming in with word that Jeff Wilson and Josh Kronfeld were worth a certain amount, the rest of us wouldn't have held out, but that was the way it panned out.

We signed on for three years and I think those of us who played for the All Blacks from 1995 were looked after much better than others. I played a few more seasons, first with the Crusaders before Wayne Smith told me I was getting too old, then Brad Meurant picked me up for the Chiefs.

My last game was in 1997 when I propped against Carl Hoeft and Kees Meeuws, and I had to swap sides during the game because my arm had gone to sleep. That confirmed it was getting tougher to stay at that level and I didn't need to go through that every week. Scrummaging wasn't the problem, but moving around the field was more of a grind, although only a few forwards beat me in the beep test. I'd been made a few offers from the UK but was happy to stay here because at 37 I thought my time was up.

When you are playing at an older age you have to do extra training and as you get older everything takes a fraction longer to get done around the farm as well. You wonder how you'll end up.

I was always going to be a farmer. I started as a stock and station agent with PGG in Seddon, Marlborough and later had a block in the Waikato and liked it out there at Ngahinapouri, but my roots were down south. I had about 500 acres of dirt at Whiterock in North Canterbury and then a couple of lease blocks growing maize, grazing dairy and finishing lambs before I was squeezed out with the dairy boom.

We moved from Whiterock to Sheffield near Darfield, but suddenly it was designated as the best place for a central plains dam. We were running sheep, beef cattle and deer and had been there only about six weeks when we were told it was one of the preferred sites for the central plains irrigation, and so we got out after about three years.

Things were starting to get going in farming, but about six years ago one of those things occurred where I had to divide things in two and now we've got a property on the north bank of the Waimakariri at the gorge where we run a Dohne Merino stud and a few cattle.

I met my wife Shane about seven years ago. After the Canterbury earthquakes, she had returned from the UK to look after the Earthquake Commission. She is originally from the Maniototo and played hockey for New Zealand for 10 years, which included the Barcelona Olympics, then worked for the New Zealand Police and was the first woman in the Armed Offenders Squad. After sport and police, she studied in the UK where she got a doctorate in sports policy then did some lecturing.

She came back to work for EQC as well as for the Prime Minister's Department and Cabinet and is now chief executive of Canterbury Rugby League and involved with other boards.

The majority of my work is on the 160-acre farm and while it is my passion, it doesn't bring in much income. It's just over lifestyle size where we run the sheep stud and a few cattle and can look after it easily. I'm an ambassador for WorkSafe, part of an ongoing push from our industry with messages about safety and wise choices on the farm.

Away from the farm, I was offered an opportunity to be involved in the media. My first taste was with Sky then I started writing a column for the *Herald on Sunday*. I felt comfortable doing those things, but what put me out of my depth was getting the chance to host a farming and rugby programme with LiveSport Radio. Every minute was a very steep learning curve and it took me some time to get into the swing of things, but it was stimulating, meeting a lot of great people involved in the rural industry and sport.

Research was fine because you are always reading and talking to people about farming trends and thinking about issues as you go about your business. Most people are confident talking about matters they are involved in, and working in radio allowed me to develop those beliefs and broaden my experience.

At the start, I travelled into a studio in Christchurch to do the show, but after the earthquake messed up the station and the city centre, we came up with a different system and I ended up working from home.

Then Mark Weldon moved into management at TV3 and as we know he shook up MediaWorks and that was the end of LiveSport after about six years. But after a couple of years away from that, I'm back with MediaWorks with Hamish McKay and Sarah Perriam hosting REX, our rural exchange programme that is broadcast on RadioLIVE at the weekends.

That role involves flying up to Auckland every Friday for a production meeting then, at the weekends, travelling into a studio in Christchurch to link up with my co-hosts. It's great to be involved again with broadcasting and the wider farming community.

I manage my own deals and have done so for most of my career, and Shane has a great eye for double-checking my ideas. I can smell or feel what's too much or not enough and loved the way John Drake did it when he was at Sky and found out what Phil Kearns was earning and asked for more.

After I stopped playing, I kept my hand in with footy and worked as a scrum advisor for both Robbie Deans at the Crusaders then my old teammate John Mitchell when he took over at the Chiefs in their 2001 campaign. Later that year, when Mitch and Robbie paired up and took over the All Blacks, I was employed as the team's scrum coach.

I did that for a couple of seasons and went on most of the

tours, including the 2003 World Cup. Helping with the All Blacks was a great experience and a privilege; it kept the pot boiling and gave me a different insight into how teams were run at the top.

That time underlined how good John Sturgeon, Colin Meads and Brian Lochore were as managers of the All Blacks in comparison to Andrew Martin and Tony Thorpe who came in later. Although we didn't have the success we wanted, I enjoyed my spell with Mitch and Robbie and working with a strong group of players and meeting blokes like Dave Hewett, Greg Somerville and Brad Thorn.

After the international stuff was over, I went back to Darfield and helped out with some of the coaching for a while and was keen to keep it at that level.

My children have always been involved in sport. My two daughters have made their mark in rowing. My eldest, Jess, rowed for about seven years in the New Zealand squad in the four and eight most of the time and is back at polytech finishing off her hospitality degree. Olivia was a reserve for the Olympics in Rio and is rowing in the double scull, while my son Duke loves playing his footy in the front row when he has time and is going well as a farmer. He has been shepherding in New Zealand and in the last year has spent time on the harvest and seeding in Western Australia and is doing some OE in Europe.

Living beside the Waimakariri River gives you plenty of options for relaxation — fishing, hunting, jetboating. I love taking the boat for several hours right up into places where you can't drive — you have to be careful, though, about running out of water.

A mountain bike has been in the shed for a while because I had a couple of knee replacements that took me out of action for a bit. A while later I found one of my crutches in the silage paddock where it must have fallen off the back of the quad bike. My knees used to ache at night and they hurt when pig-hunting and walking down hills, but that pain's gone now.

I like going to watch club rugby and usually catch the All Blacks on TV, but I don't like going into the stadium; it's just an awful place. Going to the opening test in the series against the Lions was great and so was the reunion and catching up with my old mates like Joe Stanley, Fitzy, Olo, Foxy and Mike Brewer and having a yak about what's happened in the 30 years since the first World Cup.

There are a couple of horses roaming around in the front paddock, but they're not suitable for the track, while breaking in a Clydesdale mare is a work in progress. You've got to keep busy. I'll go hunting for some venison if the freezer is empty, and I like making salamis, hams and prosciutto.

When the seasons allow, we buy lambs and keep them for about eight months to put some weight on, shear them then sell them in August or September. All my investment is tied up in the land, but it's a good life and I wouldn't want to change it.

JUSTIN MARSHALL

Justin Marshall was generally the All Blacks' first-choice halfback in a career spanning 1995 to 2005. He racked up 24 tries in 81 tests. He played for the Crusaders in Super Rugby and represented Southland and Canterbury. He later had a long stint in Europe, playing for Leeds Tykes, Ospreys, Montpellier and Saracens clubs.

Talk to anyone who has played for the All Blacks or at the high levels and you know as soon as you leave these shores that's it, the end of playing some of your best rugby alongside the greatest players you'll ever play with, with the utmost respect to what happens in the northern hemisphere.

It's a reluctant departure and it takes a while to cut through that. Every player goes through the same teething process of initially trying to change the world and saying we should play rugby this way and then accepting that's the way they do it.

I signed for a team that was not one of the giants in European rugby, but the challenge at Leeds really motivated me. I'd been lucky at the Crusaders where we'd won a lot of trophies and been successful, and I had that experience of winning regularly.

Leeds were strugglers, but the chance of going somewhere and trying to make a difference really appealed to me. We had a fabulous first year in 2006, and I made some mates who I'm still really friendly with. We played way too much rugby for the type of conditions we ran into, but often we walked away from matches after playing Leicester or Sale and crowds would say that's the best game we've seen all year.

We decided to play well and had a positive mindset and it was very enjoyable. Yet we still got relegated.

I played for Leeds, Ospreys, Montpellier and Saracens and, of that lot, perhaps my time at Ospreys was the most enjoyable. My wife Nicole cried for the best part of a week when we left Wales for Montpellier; she didn't want to go. She had settled really well, as we had in Leeds, and the Welsh people were fabulous and passionate. We had a great house we were renting in Swansea — not quite in Graham Henry's league — and our daughter Lucia was born there, while our boys Lachlan and Fletcher were born in New Zealand.

I bumped into a lot of players who went to one club and stayed, while I went to four and experienced different parts of Europe. The French offered up something very different again, in a beautiful part of the world on the Med but with few English-speaking teammates, and it was the most difficult job rugby-wise and I struggled with that.

In 2010 I was nearing the end, but you don't think it's coming. It's in the back rather than the front of your mind when you are fit and running around and happy. I still enjoyed playing, although I was also very mindful that I wasn't enjoying training, which was getting harder and more tedious, and as a pro there are 15 or so training sessions with gym work and physio sessions outside the team runs to prepare for one game. It starts to drain you.

At one stage, BBC Wales approached me to do some commentary. The camera has never bothered me — and people will smirk at that I know — but I never felt intimidated and I was never one not to put my foot in it as a player. I remember we were playing Fiji and I said if we don't put 70 points on them that's a bad day at the office for us and people read an arrogance into that. We were in the changing room thinking we should win by that amount, but when you see the tone of that comment, it never looks good in print.

I have given some interesting camera moments — one you'll recall in Dunedin where I was not happy about being subbed and another in Christchurch where I did my sternum.

I began doing stories for the BBC going race-car driving with Shane Williams and surfing with James Hook, interviewing George Gregan when he was at Toulon, and Andrew Mehrtens was there as well. I was a regular studio panellist on a show called *Scrum Five* with analysis and observation and a bit of banter; commentary wasn't a part of it at that stage.

Their instructions were to just be yourself and I have stuck with that, so when we do rehearsals for Sky here I won't give answers because I'd rather be spontaneous and be myself than use prepared lines.

I had done commentary with Sky UK and Andrew Fyfe, who was here with Sky in New Zealand, heard me and thought I could be a replacement for John Drake who sadly had passed away. He thought I would be a good fit and asked about my interest, but I was still on contract for another season with Saracens.

There are two things I remember like nothing else in my career.

I remember every bloody minute of my first All Blacks test and then the day I was driving to the biggest club rugby final in England at Twickenham when Saracens were playing Leicester Tigers and I looked out the bus window and saw a pub in Richmond called the Picture and Piano. It was a 23-degree day in London in April and everyone was sitting out on the grass banks having a beer and I wished I was sitting there with them without the stress of this big game.

Here I was going to one of the biggest games in my life and I was in a mental state I'd never been in before about an hour before kick-off. I recall standing in the middle of Twickenham about three hours later and feeling dissatisfied because we lost a game we should have won, and I knew that was going to be my last game of rugby.

I'd made up my mind about Sky's approach. They said come back and do a bit of work and play out your last year with Saracens, but I did not want to do just a bit of work.

The reality of retiring did not sit comfortably when you were talking bits and pieces. If Sky was prepared to offer me a contract, I was prepared to retire, which was a hard word to say and I did not want to leave having lost a game we should have won.

I told Nicole I could handle another year, but this was an opportunity to stop and move into another part of my life. It was too good an offer and if I didn't take it, someone else would. As much as I wanted to keep playing, it was an avenue out of the game and a chance to get back home and a heck of a good way to find out if I could do the work because I didn't know what else I was going to do. It was a massive shift and it had to be done.

Sky put their balls on the line for me and that was huge. I had played a lot of rugby and ran out onto Wembley with all my kids and had nothing left to achieve.

It was all set up, but the reality was I was going into the unknown and it would have been the same going into any other job as well.

We got home to Christchurch about July and I covered my first test in August when the All Blacks played the Wallabies in Hong Kong and James O'Connor kicked a sideline conversion to win. I had worked on one commentary before that in the UK, but this was the All Blacks. My instructions were: this button does this, that button does that, and, remember, you are always live — good luck! That was it.

Tony Johnson called that game. I was very nervous, but he gave me good advice, which was if in doubt don't say anything or if you are not sure let the pictures do the talking. I enjoyed it and it was a cracking game of rugby and a great one to get my teeth into.

I sought out some feedback and knew I was entering media circles where I had probably pissed off a lot of people when I was playing. Later in my career, I was difficult to interview because it became tedious having to front for those chats, so people probably saw a side that was not really me but rather someone wondering 'Do I have to go through this again?'

There was a lot of repair work needed. I had moaned my arse off about night rugby and that was all driven by television, so I made sure I was humble and the boy in the organisation who had to learn, and I was keen to do that because I enjoyed it.

It was a strange year because we got back in July and the first Canterbury earthquakes hit in September, so it was an awful introduction back to New Zealand. When the first quake hit, I was away playing in a golf tournament and we were not affected much, but in the following February it hit us really badly in Sumner and, again, I was away working in Auckland.

It was awful for Nicole because we were living on the hill and she couldn't get to the kids who were stuck at school, and there was talk of a tsunami and people were killed by falling debris.

Our kids weren't coping well, so we moved to Queenstown. We didn't want to move, but our children were at the stage where the eldest should have gone to counselling. He still struggles with the effects of it all.

I switched from being a professional rugby player in Europe for nearly six years to a new job and then the earthquakes hit, our kids went to new schools twice, we moved to Queenstown at the start of 2011 and it all seemed surreal when I looked at the calendar of what we'd done as a family since I retired in July. All I knew was I had to have an airport near me.

Coming from Mataura, I'd always dreamed of living in Queenstown because it was only two hours away from anywhere and we travelled a fair bit. We rented initially because of our issues in Christchurch, but now we are building at Jacks Point so I can be on the golf course. Nicole and I have designed the house and have good synergy about most things and have enjoyed the project.

There have been a number of spin-offs from working at Sky. The media side of my work has broadened to radio and print with a ghosted column in the *New Zealand Herald* and writing a column for *Rugby News*, which is not easy — fair play to you guys doing it all the time.

Then there is the corporate work with banks, real estate companies, hosting lunches and dinners, which takes up as much time as television. At the start of each season, Sky gives you a roster of games, so you know what you are up for and can plan most of your year. I look after my own schedule and prefer it that way and can be as busy or flexible as we want. I see my kids a lot at trainings for their sport but sadly miss most of their games at the weekends.

I really enjoy what I do and feel very privileged to do it. I'm lucky, and all of it is still very enjoyable. One thing grates, though — having to be at venues so early before kick-off, milling around and waiting for around four hours. As a player I hated being there even an hour before kick-off. The atmosphere at tests is a level up and as a former All Black I love watching the team play, but working in every game is similar. I'm as happy commentating on a lower-division provincial game as a test because I love it.

I came into the job thinking if Richie McCaw comes into the side of a ruck I'm not going to pretend it didn't happen. Everyone else sees that and it would be silly pretending he didn't do it. The rest of the world has seen it and just because we are New Zealanders doesn't mean we should turn a blind eye to it. That mindset annoys some people who ask whether I have a chip on my shoulder, but I am trying to tell the facts — the All Blacks are offside or whatever — and that is just logic and common sense.

If a player is having a bad day, there's nothing worse than a commentator highlighting that point but, again, you can't deceive the viewer, so you can say he's not playing to his usual high standards. That irked me when I was playing and I wanted commentators to ignore me, but now I appreciate what they are doing; it is not personal and they are telling us what is happening.

I've been working for Sky for six years or so and would love to stay in this job because rugby is my passion and if I wasn't doing this work, I'd be watching every game anyway. Rugby is in my blood and the fact I'm able to work in it is as much a godsend as playing.

The reality is the game evolves and although I'm getting older and further away from the game it doesn't mean you can't still see things. There's so much going on in the television world; there's always speculation about rights being negotiated and how the future will look. While it is not as fickle a business as being a player, there is always some uncertainty about the future. To a degree, you feel that.

Like rugby, you don't sign contracts for more than three or four years and that is your future. It is not long-term solidity, but you want to concentrate on what you are doing now. I don't need to give myself an ulcer and don't need to be a worrier like my old man who frets about everything.

It's good to have some vision to work out how you would cope if things go pear-shaped, but I don't agonise about it. Corporate work is a good backstop and I'm comfortable talking about my favourite subject, which is me, so it's an easy thing to do. They want to hear about times behind the All Blacks lines and we reminisce and it's a conversation.

I'm a fisherman and a big fan of catching blue cod. I love water-skiing and if it's active I'm into it — I snow ski, play squash and golf and keep busy with the kids. As long as it's competitive and sport, it's fine by me. The boys carry my name and every son of an All Black has to deal with the good and bad of that. It doesn't seem to sit badly with them.

In our free time, we go on family holidays to Riverton, Fiji or Noosa and, of course, it's always great just staying at home. Golf is a good chance to catch up with mates like Olo

Brown, Christian Cullen or Gregan and I'm an ambassador at Jacks Point and have played Valderrama in Spain, Celtic Manor in Wales and Muirfield in Scotland, which are just great experiences. I'd love to get on and play Augusta. I'm busy, rugby is all-encompassing and life is great.

KEVEN MEALAMU

Keven Mealamu was an All Black from 2002 to 2015, playing in 132 tests and scoring 12 test tries. He also had a long career in Super Rugby with the Blues and Chiefs and represented Auckland.

I still remember having a talk with Steve Hansen in 2012 about what I had to do to get to the 2015 Rugby World Cup because that was the target to end my career. One year was a long time at test level and it seemed a long way to another World Cup.

It was actually nice to say, 'This is my goal; this is what I am aiming at,' but it was also an unusual feeling because you knew that would be it. But it was about having an eye on things after rugby, ideas I'd thought about outside rugby, and around then I started to look a bit deeper into what I might do and what that might look like.

My last few years of playing were about putting some hard work into making sure that today looks like today, which is time at my gym, some work I do with New Zealand Rugby and taking some of the leadership skills I learned through rugby and using that in the corporate world. That part has been especially interesting, as the pressure to present a programme has a similar feeling to running out for a rugby test.

Speaking with Steve, he always came across as someone with something sharp to say. I've spent a lot of time with him and had many good conversations, and our chats were about what I needed to work on to stay in the All Blacks group. They were about getting good clarity around my role, which started to change in the team and on the field.

It was a crossover time and if you don't look at that the right way it can have a negative impact on your game and what you are doing. When you get that sorted, you can play some really good footy if you come on as a sub in the last quarter when things count a lot.

I'm from an era when you wanted to play the whole game, but we talked about being adaptable and adjusting and a change of emphasis with an extended squad. Being a leader never left my game, but I needed to make sure how the other parts fitted in around that.

It wasn't about being at peace with the role; it was more working out how best I was going to carry it out. It was different, learning how to watch a game from the bench and working out where best to make an impact.

It sunk in when I walked off Twickenham in 2015 after a really good performance in the World Cup final. The cool thing for a lot of us throughout that final week was not talking about how this would be our last All Blacks match. It was about winning a game. That was our sole focus.

After that match there was a great sense of accomplishment. After the 2011 final there was relief, but four years later it was an amazing feeling about what we had achieved.

It wasn't easy. When things went well and we had a really good team and leaders, it was about keeping those standards high and making sure we went through everything instead of brushing over any areas.

That last All Blacks jersey from 2015 is hanging up in my wardrobe and my last pair of boots are there too. I'm still figuring out what I want to do with a lot of my gear. I wore a new pair of boots for the final then cleaned them, took out the sprigs and brought them home. I've never worn that jersey again and won't.

Some of the awesome things about rugby are the pathways it offers and the people you get to meet and the range of ideas you encounter. I work for Barfoot & Thompson real estate company, through my connection with Peter Thompson who has run his successful business and has strong family values and is a good people person — as well as being a really good rugby man. Even though we've been in different industries, it helps to watch how he works.

This is my tenth year with Barfoots, illustrating their books and raising money for Starship Hospital. I thought I would have more opportunities to work on their books, but my time is restricted.

When I was little, my grandparents always had artwork up around the house, and my mother and sister are artists. It's a hobby for me and I don't think I'm that good, but I love it. I don't mind painting, although I'm not as accurate as I am with pencil or the new pro-markers, which are like drawing with a vivid. They are cool to use and have different-sized heads and you can blend all sorts of colours.

I still sit up at the bench at home and draw. It's one of those things that you can't pick a time to do; you have to be in the mood and have clear ideas. If you're on a roll, you keep moving because there are lots of other times when you have artist's block or lack inspiration. I don't carve and I don't have any ambition to do any sculpture, but Barfoots auctioned off one of my paintings and there was a bit of pressure there to come up with something of decent quality.

I am fairly freestyle and might have a few other images around the main picture, though it's different if you are drawing from a photo. I grew up in the comic era with all those characters, so form rather than colour interests me.

I studied arts and graphics at Aorere College and worked as an apprentice signwriter at Greg Owens' shop in Pakuranga for 18 months doing signs, billboards, cars and windows and a lot of cleaning, picking up rubbish and mixing paint before an NPC contract then Super Rugby came along and I left.

One of the toughest issues now is getting an invitation to go down to watch the Blues and knowing where the boundary is — wanting to go down and see the boys but being concerned I'm hanging on. Maybe next year will be easier because you want to stay connected.

I miss the mateship, the banter and the competition but not the playing. There were a few rugby offers, including some good ones, but I was happy to finish when I did.

Richie McCaw and I would talk about our good fortune in being able to choose when we would finish rather than having someone making that decision for us. It's best to look at the whole picture rather than isolate it to one year or game.

After rugby, I always knew I would be busy supporting my family. That is a priority along with working at something I enjoy rather than it being a daily slog. It had to mean something, which is why we love having our Fit60 gym where we can look after our family and at the same time help people get fit and improve their outlook on life.

It's a group training gym at Takanini that used to be a panelbeating shop. We got the lease in mid-2014 and opened in early 2015, so I was training there and rehabbing. It gave me a balance outside rugby and if your mind is fresh it keeps everything else fresh.

I sourced information from friends who were in the industry and put into practice some of the things I felt might be a point of difference from other gyms. We needed good staff, a lawyer and accountant, and there was so much lateral thinking required to achieve what you see in front of you.

It was eye-opening stuff to discover all the processes and do it ourselves whereas in the All Blacks, off the field, everything was done for us. We made lots of decisions on the rugby track, though, and doing that helps once your career is over.

We hold three or four classes a day for six days. We're closed on Sunday and that's time for the family because my son is in secondary school and my daughter will be there soon, and that's part of the balance.

I'm in most days. If not, my wife Latai is there or someone else in the family and it's great working alongside someone with the same values and vision and getting to change people's lives or take them in another direction. It's another form of discipline and we realise it's a time of our lives when we have to put the work in.

My work as an ambassador with New Zealand Rugby varies. Some of it is very challenging and is looking to initiate change rather than being the foot soldier. It's a new role NZR initiated and I feel blessed to be involved. It covers so many things, but we have to make sure it is all current and that's the part I like.

It's called 'Be in This Space' and it's fresh. We try to plan a block of work for a month and adapt from there. It is run nationwide, but a lot of our time is based from Counties through Auckland to North Harbour.

Learning new paths is pretty cool, especially where it's a different kind of leadership — planning more than leading by service. A lot of it is based around mental health and it does not just cover rugby. Anyone in the community can log into our website to learn about the signs that someone is not going so well.

We are also looking at pathways after school and that's a massive job. The better you are organised the better it is. We have many schools coming to us and asking to get involved. I usually visit them with someone so we can bounce ideas off each other and check how we are going.

I'm a determined person and I'm not sure where that tenacity comes from, although Brendan Cannon reckoned I could have been a cage fighter. I come from a long line of men who could look after themselves and had a warrior spirit. They were hard-working and never gave up. Dad was tough, very humble and quiet but not someone to mess with and he still tells me off.

I've got a reputation for being polite when I played, but also someone who was not to be crossed because that's when I do everything for my teammates. I learned a lot as a youngster from many very hard men, although rugby was even more rugged in the era before me.

My Catholic faith is a family thread. I grew up with those beliefs and we try to pass that on without forcing it on people. It's a way of living your life and conducting yourself and having that relationship with God, whatever that looks like.

I'm learning more about my Samoan heritage and what that means and how to live in both worlds. My children are part Samoan, Tongan and European and we talk about perceptions and how we view things. Values run through everyone — common values. Mum is New Zealand-born Samoan, Dad is Samoan, so we keep those connections strong.

Sadly, there is no great encouragement for a Pacific Island side in the search for a better Super Rugby formula. Japan is there, but that does not seem quite right to me and it would be awesome to include an Island side, although I don't know what that would look like or how it can happen. The more time I spend on the other side you look at how it all works and wonder about the problems getting a sustainable Pacific side, which would help grow the game. It's a long-term project, but I'm not sure it's possible because of the challenges. It'll take some good people and brains to be around that conversation.

Maybe my hero Michael Jones can work something out. He was such a magnificent rugby player — he tackled me so hard when we first played against each other — and achieves such a lot in all the other parts of his life. He's a smart man who had two massive injuries then adapted and has such a strong character. He's like many of the guys I was around at the top level; their actions showed me the way to perform. I work alongside him quite a lot now.

Giving and serving is my life and you get plenty back. I love what I'm doing.

GLEN OSBORNE

After he debuted in 1995, Glen Osborne featured at fullback for the World Cup but spent most of the rest of his career until 1999 on the wing. He played 19 tests and ran in 11 test tries. He played for the Chiefs and Hurricanes in Super Rugby and represented Wanganui and North Harbour. He also featured in the New Zealand Sevens team and played a season and a half in France with Biarritz club and four seasons in Japan with Ricoh.

After leaving the All Blacks I played in France, for North Harbour then four years in Japan, which was one of the most exciting things I've ever done. It was beautiful. The people are kind and respectful, they have the most beautiful wairua and are such genuine people. You deal with Japanese people here, but they are completely different in their own environment.

I was playing for Ricoh, based just out of Setagaya in Tokyo, and we had Eroni Clarke, Paul Feeney was our coach, and there was Brandon Jackson, Norm Maxwell and a few Aussies. I've still got the club record for points in a year.

My wife Kylee and I put the girls straight into Japanese school because by the time we got there my eldest, Arianna, was at primary school, my youngest Mako was three and they picked up the language in a few months. They became fluent very quickly and could tell jokes in Japanese; that's how good they were.

I picked up Japanese better than French because the pronunciation is similar to Maori, and because I loved it I made more effort to learn it, going to night school for lessons.

In 2004 I told the club I would give them one more year because my body was too tired. They said okay, okay.

I just wanted to retire and they offered me another contract to stay. I was sore and didn't have the heart to do it any more. They offered me more money, but I wanted to go home. They didn't understand, so I told them to send some guys over to see me in New Zealand then they'd understand why I wanted to be back here.

When we finally left, they all came out to the airport with their children and were all crying and singing; it was very emotional.

I flew in on a Wednesday and on Thursday I was working at Maori TV on *Code*. A good friend of mine, Bailey Mackey, helped me out a lot and it was hard work being a presenter and doing that front work but Jenny-May Clarkson, who worked with me, is my best mate in television. She was fantastic. Whenever I got in strife she'd say, 'Don't worry, Oz, no one's going to die,' and she was my rock during my TV career. I did *Code* for a couple of years, then *The 3rd Half* with Willie Lose and Buck Shelford before I had my own show, *Bring Your Boots, Oz*, and I took over *Hunting Aotearoa* in my last year.

In 2011 I fronted the Rugby World Cup for the hour before a game and with a panel afterwards, and then I spent the best part of a decade at Maori TV when we were living at Omaha, north of Auckland.

At the same time, I bought a butchery in Matakana and that was trying to kill two birds with one stone. I had my hunting goals and knew if I bought the butchery I would have all the dog tucker I needed and with all the pigs I caught, I could do my own salami and pork at home, plus get experience in another side of the business.

I will say having the butchery was really, really hard simply because I was not a qualified butcher. While I knew how to cut up most meat, that wasn't being a butcher. One of my best mates up there, Matthew Oldfield, was my home-kill man, so he worked for me and showed me how to do it.

We had a home-kill business and that meat had to be labelled and kept separate from the shop stuff, which was meat we had to buy in. Our market was all local and we were really busy around the Rodney district.

Eventually, I was working three days a week at Maori TV and I said I couldn't work every day. It was long hours working out how to make a business run, and I came to the conclusion that I wanted to go home.

I got really homesick. It's hard to explain. I've always wanted to go home, but at the end of 2012 it got to a point where I wasn't happy. I looked at the bigger picture and one day I said to my wife, 'Babe, I just want to go home. I don't want to be in this lifestyle any more. I don't like it.'

We sold the house, sold the business, everything.

My wife is from Taranaki and suggested we go there, but I said she'd chosen to go to France first then Japan and this was my call. I said if I moved I was going home to Whanganui.

A few weekends later we went home for a trip and looked at some places to buy. We saw about five or six, but there was one we fell in love with straight away and I told the real estate agent that we would make an offer.

My older brother Charles, who is a builder and played for Wanganui, started work on the new 300-square-metre house and I helped him between shows. Kylee liked the house and it took a bit more persuasion to get her to believe it was all going to turn out well. It's on the edge of town in Westmere, so it's not far to get to work or to other places around the district.

I was born in Ngamatapouri about an hour inland, as you go towards Waverley and Waitotora and then turn inland and go way up there. All my life I was out in the sticks and loved it.

It's the freedom, never having neighbours and being happy in my own company. I met Kylee when I came to play in Auckland and met her at the rugby club when she was up on work experience from Taranaki. She was at TVNZ working on *Mai Time* as one of the first presenters before working as a reporter.

Once the house was ready, we moved down. My eldest daughter Arianna had finished at Mahurangi College and went to Toi Whakaari in Wellington to learn directing and acting, and we sent our younger daughter Mako to Wanganui Collegiate, which is a wonderful school. She's now studying business and commerce in Wellington; she's got her mother's abilities and Kylee pushed the girls.

Moving gave me another chance to have a go at getting into the police force. I wanted to try when I was 23, but we were playing professional rugby then and weren't allowed to work anywhere else.

I was thinking I was too old and had maybe missed my chance at doing something I'd always wanted to do. The core values of the police are very similar to what you need in rugby. There is a strong correlation of professionalism, teamwork, empathy, respect and time management. I came from an All Blacks side that had those highest standards in the world then went into TV where, again, you have to have high standards otherwise you just don't last.

Transferring those disciplines made sense and all my life I was taught about hard work by my dad. I was a cheeky kid, but I was disciplined, and I worked hard for my dad, milking and shearing, so that work ethic was there for me.

All my life I have wanted to be a role model so my nieces and nephews can see there is more to life. I wanted to stand out and I knew that being a police officer you had that chance, not because of the blue uniform but as someone who upholds values and is professional. It's a wonderful career, and the values are as high as I believe All Blacks' values are.

There was no age limit and when I went in I was the oldest by far in my group, but I easily passed the fitness testing. Then I applied for interviews about 2015 and the fitness trials were the easiest thing of the lot for me. Next step was the hardest — the psychometric tests with abstract, numerical and written exams. I hadn't studied for 30 years and you have to pass that before you can go to police college. I spent months studying hard because I knew if you didn't pass you had to wait six months or more for another shot.

I wanted to get it right the first time. Three weeks after the exam I was driving my car and got a phone call saying I had passed and I was so excited, I swore; 'You're f***ing kidding me!' and the lady said, 'No, Mr Osborne.' I had passed but needed to upskill some papers because getting into Porirua Police College was apparently much harder.

I waited six months to go there and then it was four months of intense study. The physical stuff was easy, but the mental strain and tension were tough.

I tried to do my training at police college without any fanfare, but as soon as they found out at Maori TV that I was there they wanted to do a documentary. I saw the police inspector and he said I didn't need any distractions — and he was so right. I didn't want to fail, so the pressure was on.

The stress was so great I spoke to my sergeant about struggling through my first mock exams when I got about 30 per cent and you needed about 70 per cent to pass. He said, 'Look, you've made the All Blacks, you been on TV and have worked hard. So this is what I want you to do . . .'

I had about 100 cue cards and he said that's too much information; bullet points are the go. I cut them down to about 25 points and that made a massive difference. I got about 74 per cent, I think, then 82 per cent in my tests, but all the way through there were exams to push us.

My good mate Stacy Lamb, who was 49 and a fitness guy too, was also stressed about the exams. We joined up with a few others to do blackboard sessions, and I was only going home to Whanganui once every three weeks because I needed to be full-time at college.

Two days before the 2016 graduation ceremony I did not know whether I had passed, then they called us into a room. Some got sent home. Congrats they told us, everyone in your class has passed; it was the first time in 14 years that had happened and that was all 60 of us in our wing.

We were laughing, crying, shouting and screaming —

brother Stacy, who's now a constable in Taranaki, was going berserk. Everyone came to the graduation, my brother and cousin and folks and, for me, it was the biggest day of my life. With rugby I knew I was reasonably good at the game and had a reasonable chance of being an All Black, but in the police I felt so proud about what I had achieved.

The ambassador for our wing was John Hart. He was there for all of us every few weeks and tried to keep it a secret. He made sure he knew all our names and encouraged me and helped me to pass. My stress levels were so high at one stage that I had to talk to the nurse, who also had psychiatric training. It wasn't embarrassing; it was to get some help for breathing and study and coping.

I got an 85 in my last exam and Stacy got 84, and we were the ones with the lowest marks at the start. I'd never had marks like that at school.

Having graduated and with my wife and kids in Whanganui and my whanau there, I wanted to work in the city and they wanted me there. I started in September 2016 and ended up in a section with the most gifted police officer in Whanganui, Zac Thornton, who's been in the force about 10 years and was with the army before that.

My role is frontline, in a car, on the street, being the eyes and connection to the community, dealing with all the stuff going on. We do frontline work, we do traffic and whatever needs doing and have about 100 police in the area. While I love the place, there is a lot of crime.

I've got lots of cousins who are in Black Power and Hells Angels, and as a police officer they know me and respect what I do, and I respect them. I love my cousins, but they took a different path. It's tough locking one of them up, but I've told them, I come from a strict family and if they commit crimes something will have to happen.

That's how it is. One thing I am very strong on is drink driving and I've told them if I ever catch you I promise you I will arrest you. You put yourself in danger, your family in danger and my cousins in danger. They know where I stand.

The worst thing to deal with is domestic violence and I see a lot of it. The hardest thing is seeing the cycle carry on from their parents to here and here and here. You see kids in houses that shouldn't be lived in and it's the young who suffer and my heart goes out to them.

It depresses me, but I am there to do a job and help people because that is the right thing to do. This is me, it is long term. You work hard to get the job you want, and I am not giving that away.

I don't watch as much footy as I used to, but I sit down with my family and we watch every All Blacks match. I also go to club rugby. I am a life member at Kaierau Rugby Club and watch them play as much as I can.

Any other spare time I go pig-hunting. My dad Charlie taught me everything about the craft; he's a workaholic still going hard out on the land and is my role model.

Training dogs is my passion and this year I took a couple of my dogs to Niue to help train guys' dogs there. I've got five at home and my favourite work is training them, developing them from pups; it's great. I go bush and I'm off. My nephew and I go pig-hunting and sometimes I take a few young cuzzies who are good kids — but at the crossroads where they could go down the wrong path — and I teach them about tracking, riding bikes, gun safety and how to cut up meat so they can look after themselves.

ARRAN PENE

As No. 8, Arran Pene played 15 tests 1992–94 and scored four test tries. He represented Otago at provincial level. He went on to a long career in Japan with Kaneka and Fukuoka Sanix Bombs clubs.

Going to the All Blacks reunion during the Lions tour and reflecting on the influence Sir John Graham — DJ — delivered through education were a couple of topical checkpoints about how we live and what the future might bring.

Normally, there are a couple of questions I like to get out of the way at rugby get-togethers and the first is: 'Are you still with so and so?' and then it's 'How's the body hanging together — and what about your general health and lifestyle?' DJ was very big on education and having a breadth of interests to keep body and mind ticking over.

I coach at under-15 level with Todd Miller at Hamilton Boys' High and I'm concerned about rugby at that level and the elite grades. Lots of Polynesian boys mature early and make sides because of that genetic advantage, but I urge the rest not to worry about making rep teams or the First XV because they have years of rugby ahead of them and if their skills are strong, they will succeed.

My sons have been through rowing and rugby systems where success is measured by the Maadi Cup and First XV results. While rowing is predominantly a white sport with a strong support system, I wonder about rugby where there are Arthur Lydiard-type principles of loading up the boys and thrashing them. You wonder what happens to them in the future.

It comes back to questions DJ would ask about having a Plan B and the importance of education. How many of these boys are thinking about apprenticeships, going into the services or perhaps on to higher education? Why do so few make it to First XV level and then fail to progress to the ITM Cup?

Who knows whether my sons will end up playing rugby at any high level, but the great thing is the comradeship and opportunities the game brings, like last year when my eldest boy Sam, who is studying in Otago, hooked up with John Timu's boy for a few beers out at Tarras. That's great; that's what life's about. Whether they play rugby or not is immaterial, but hopefully they have a few more clues than their father.

I was in the All Blacks frame for the 1995 World Cup but probably played my way out because I had an injury. Maybe it was a bit of immaturity at that stage, and when you are involved with a team you never want to give a sucker a break, but it didn't happen and my good mate Jamie Joseph came back to get into the tournament team.

I was probably still sulking and wanted to have another go. In 1996 the All Blacks were going to tour South Africa and they weren't going to take young players. We had a chance, but it was Jamie who said, 'If we are not in the starting XV we are vulnerable. Let's go and secure our future,' and I thought about that and agreed.

We both went to Japan and I had 10 seasons over there. It was fantastic. It secured our future financially, we made lifelong relationships and the contract helped me build a business ethic too. I worked for pharmaceutical company Kaneka, based at Takasago near Osaka, who were into protein powders and supplements and were interested in using whey protein which is a by-product here.

My contract was a mix of playing and working for the company, a more encompassing deal where even if the team wasn't going well, I would go in and translate documents and proof-read deals and you learned a great deal about Japan, the way they did business and all the language around that. Now they only offer professional playing deals and can cut you after a few seasons.

We were in the second wave of players who went to Japan behind people like Andrew McCormick who went up there with Rob Gordon and worked for very traditional companies. That was when you put in 40 to 50 hours around your footy, whereas we were more part-time. McCormick was known as Mr Japan there in terms of rugby and Rob Gordon now lives in France and works for Airbus. Our move was around the time of others like Laurie O'Reilly, Herb Schuler, Jamie, the Bachops and Marty Brooke, but a decade up there is unheard of now.

It was good for my wife Sonia and me, and we had a lot of time with our kids, whereas in professional rugby in New Zealand you wouldn't get that so much. We travelled and learned a new way of life, then it was time for the kids to come home and to enjoy this country and its lifestyle and get into some rough and tumble with their cousins.

Sam is down at Otago, Zac is in his second to last year at Hamilton Boys', Ned is Year 11 and Sophie is in Year 9 at Diocesan School for Girls. They were all born in New Zealand, but the first three got to experience a little of what life was like in Japan.

I don't know if it was the Scottish conservative upbringing you get in Otago that rubbed off on me, which is not bad for a Maori boy from Raglan, but Japan was all about getting a deposit on a house and making sure we were set up for our return.

My degree was a piece of paper that says you can apply yourself for three or four years and then you go into the real world and learn what life's about. As a football player who played tests, you back yourself, so I came home and worked for a couple of years. I've talked to a lot of players and others who served overseas with the army and it takes you a good couple of years to settle back into the different pace and style of life in New Zealand.

We had a nice lifestyle when we came back to Raglan. Sonia worked in a pharmacy and I worked on the rubbish trucks for a year or so, which was fantastic because I enjoyed the physical side of it, and the kids were small and went to a country school. Originally, we thought about going back to Dunedin, but with kids being a big part of the equation the grandparents come into it too, and Sonia's parents are from up north at Kawakawa and mine were in the Waikato, which is why we stayed.

Sonia and I met in my first year at university at Waikato because I didn't get into Dunedin. My notes weren't too flash and I asked if I could borrow hers. Then she switched to Wellington to do pharmacy and I went to Dunedin to do phys-ed.

After a couple of years back from Japan and staying in Raglan, I decided to have a crack at a Speight's Ale House. I'd been looking for an opportunity and thought there was a gap in the market in Hamilton and we've got a strong location near the motels and close to Waikato Stadium.

A good mate, Peter Kean, was at Lion Breweries and Mark Scully started the original Speight's in Dunedin. Most of us played rugby and had some connection with Otago University or Dunedin — Greg Cooper worked in Hawke's Bay, Justin Cullen at Petone and Greg Halford in Wellington.

My experience of the hospitality industry was limited, but part of being in Dunedin for many years was taking on some of the values of Speight's, and coming from a Maori background I've worked in kitchens, been on the tea-towels and that manaaki or looking after people is important and something we still do. Sometimes it takes a while to learn lessons, but the hospitality game has taught me to never underestimate the power of putting food on the table and having time with your kids.

People tell me I run my pub like a rugby team. My kitchen is my forward pack and all the good-looking guys and girls — the backs — are out the front, but I tell them that forwards win games, so if we don't get the food out on time and it's not good and hot then we lose. Culture is a big part of sport and business and the best teams I played with have a fantastic culture.

There are about 18 Speight's bars around the country and we started in 2009 when we converted a big glass-walled car company building on Anglesea Street to the Speight's style with the kauri bar, copper air-conditioning ducts, and schist and weatherboard exterior. We have a licensing trade agreement and paid for the fit-out — that's your fee in — and then you get on with it.

People perceive us as a franchise but we're not and we're left to develop our own systems. However, if I've got any questions I can ring a number of guys around the country or go and see how they operate. Everyone shares and adapts, although there are certain things that people expect when they go to any Speight's Ale House in the country, whether it is the chowder, shanks or other core items. When the ale houses were set up they were for selling booze and the first ones had tiny kitchens, but booze is on the decline and food is a big part of the experience now.

When the Lions were on tour here it was manic, bedlam. We want punters here till about 11 or 12 o'clock then they start moving downtown. We are open seven days and my business partner Phil Dunn and I will be here at busy times, but I get most weekends off now. At the start we worked very long hours, but if we were still doing that we would not be efficient.

We have a North Island Speight's Ale House group and national conferences, and a lot of guys use mentors like Peter Kean, while having an accountant like Brett Craies is a key part — you live and die by your staff. We employ a lot of students and three or four full-timers and understand that hospitality is a way to a means. We want our staff to go on to bigger and better things, so if we can guide them and they learn a few skills along the way that's great.

We had a few quieter years around the recession and when we lost the V8 races down here. Hospitality is a tough industry. We pay our way; we are not breaking records, but we have a lifestyle and the Waikato has a robust economy. We have some competition in town, but we are out of the CBD where people can park up, have a meal, get a drink and then if they want to kick on they can go elsewhere.

Spare time is spent with the family, chasing the kids at sport and coaching schoolboy rugby. Sam is making the transition from loose forward to hooker, Zac is in the junior New Zealand softball team, Ned is in under 15s and is rowing too and Sophie plays netball where the spectators are more vicious than the rugby crowds!

We have a big boys' walking group where about 23 of us meet at the pub at 5.30 am every Saturday and go for two hours, then have a cup of tea and solve all the problems of the world. We call it the High Performance Maori Walking Group. I do cross-fit as well and still do a bit of running.

I'm trying to keep fit and behaving myself after spending the first 40 years going hard, but you still have to live life. I played at 120 kg and have kept it to about 125 kg and make sure I go to the doctor every year to get the warrant of fitness check.

We'll be staying here for a while, although I've always liked primary industry — *Country Calendar* is still one of my favourite TV programmes — and my in-laws have a bit of dirt up north and I could see myself up there. We have to wait until the kids are out of the high school system. Half of me thinks about going back down south to Dunedin, then I give myself an uppercut, especially as grandparents are still a big part of the equation.

I'm chairman of the Waikato Maori Rugby Committee that helps with governance and keeps the books in order, while I also catch up with the Otago boys most years. We used to do that at a test match, but that was a waste of time because we would end up having a court session in the middle of the game so now we pick a non-rugby day and go somewhere small.

TAINE RANDELL

Taine Randell's All Blacks career spanned 1995 to 2002 and included 51 tests and 12 test tries. He played for the Highlanders in Super Rugby and represented Otago. He later played for English club Saracens.

I was made redundant by All Blacks coach John Mitchell in 2003, even though I was his captain the year before, and I was playing for the Barbarians in the UK that season when Bart Campbell, an agent, said, 'Come and meet this guy.'

It turned out to be Nigel Wray who owned Saracens and he made a compelling offer for me to play for the club. My wife Jo had worked in the UK for a couple of years and said, 'Come on, let's go and do it again.' Super Rugby had finished and it was sunny in the UK, which was a nice change from normally being there in November–December.

I'd been picked for the All Blacks in 2002 but knew my days were numbered. I'd never really wanted to play in the UK but had such a good time there in 2003 I said, 'Okay, let's go.' I had a couple of seasons at Saracens: the first was good, the second a slog, but we did really well and qualified for the European Cup.

Jo had a great job with Airwaves, a communications company who were part of O2, and during the six weeks off-season I worked for Barclays Banking but didn't like it.

I went for an interview at a brokerage firm and spoke to someone for about 10 minutes. My interview was winding down and appeared to be going nowhere. The boss initially said he had no intention of giving me a job; he just wanted to meet an All Black! He was a paratrooper, an outstanding guy. Suddenly, he said, 'Let's talk wages. When can you start?'

So in my last year playing rugby I worked three afternoons a week at Tradition Financial Services in the heart of London. I dealt in oil futures with three clients. There were six of us on a desk and our clients were banks, speculators, airlines and petrol companies. We'd have three or four screens each, several phones with noise all around, buying and selling crude in a version of the stock exchange and money market.

When I started the oil price was 32 bucks, later it went to 149 per barrel and when I left it was in the 70s and then went back down to 34. Halfway through 2008 we went on holiday with our two kids in Turkey, it was pissing down and Jo broke down at the airport and said, 'I've been in Dunedin for 12 years, here for seven, it's cold and I'm going home. You can come if you want.'

I handed in my resignation on the day Lehman Brothers went bust. I stayed for another six weeks because I wasn't going to a competitor, whereas normally they kicked you out the door straight away. Jo went early because her mother was crook, but I handed my clients over and went on the lunch and booze circuit.

We took a few months to get back to New Zealand and travelled through Italy, Egypt, Turkey and Dubai with Lanson, who is 13 now, and Tori who is 11 — while we also have Tenara now who is seven.

Trading was a real mix. We had a Greek Cypriot woman who looked after all the Indians and Pakistanis, while some tech guys and I were in charge of all the pisshead English buffoons, the hooray Henry set who were good boys, gamblers and very social.

One of the deals we did was over a long lunch with Macquarie Bank and BP when we were arguing about prices. We signed on the beer coaster, a guy with a rickshaw drew up, one guy gave him a card and some instructions and half an hour later the deal was done for 100,000 barrels of oil. Behind all the nonsense, they were brilliant mathematicians.

It took a while to get tuned into the futures markets and how the oil price is linked to currency, whereas in New Zealand the focus is agricultural with dairy futures and carbon credits and that sort of stuff.

We wandered our way back home and thought we'd have enough money to exist for a while, but that wasn't the case. We fluffed around for a few years and lived at the beach at Waimarama, 25 kilometres east of Hastings, which is a great spot but travelling to town each day wasn't good. Then we moved to live with Jo's parents on their farm for three months before buying Alan Duff's house, which was about a third built and put out to tender when he went bust.

I don't know that we'd do it again. We are still there on a couple of acres, but it was a massive project to finish.

Jo was still working for her London firm, the kids were just starting school and I had no idea what I wanted to do because there was no money market in Hawke's Bay.

In 2009, we were sorting out the assets of my grandmother

who was a Maori landowner and thought about this emissions trading scheme thing.

A lot of Maori blocks are in forestry and when we were in London trading oil, the emissions trading scheme started in Europe in 2005 and by the time I finished three years later, you could buy oil and carbon credits to offset that, so I knew quite a bit about how the European scheme worked. There were some similarities in New Zealand.

We ended up doing a few things in the carbon credit space and that's when I started a little company specialising in carbon credits. New Zealand has obligations through the Kyoto Protocol to keep to certain levels in what is the biggest agreement governing climate change. There are lots of rules and there is a level New Zealand has to achieve. If we produce more carbon, we have to buy credits out of the international market, and if we produce less the government can sell our allocation.

The Kyoto Protocol gives the government 64 million credits annually, so at the end of the year we have to account for that number. If we produce 65 million we have go to the market to buy from someone who doesn't produce as much carbon, and if we produce only 60 million, the government can sell the rest of the allocation to, say, Japan.

Every tree grown by landowners absorbs a certain amount of carbon dioxide, and for every ton they absorb there is a credit, which is basically an internal exchange. So the carrot is you reduce the amount of carbon by becoming more efficient; otherwise you have to buy carbon credits to offset it.

The incentive for landowners is to grow more trees because that is the international way of offsetting credits and we have our Maori land. I had a vague idea how it worked globally, but in New Zealand no one had a clue.

The first timeframe was 2012 so we were flat out going around mainly Maori blocks of land to explain to them how the scheme worked. Te Puni Kokiri now has just under 40 million credits in its account.

We also worked for our company Tipu Green and it was an awesome job travelling from one end of the country to another seeing some stunning regions. We worked with Maori trusts in Te Kuiti, Taumarunui, Ruatoria and Hicks Bay where people are often dirt poor but have great natural food resources.

I was stunned. I've become a bit of a greenie, a bit worryingly, but commercially it is irresponsible to do it any other way. We have to do things differently not because of the touchy-feely thing but commercially it makes sense. We have other clients we are still looking after, but our main job with Maori land blocks is done.

Then I joined Ngati Kahungunu as a director in 2010. They are the third biggest iwi in the country and representatives are elected by the marae. In 2007 as part of the fisheries settlement they started a company that had to be managed independently of the iwi and I sit on the board.

Ngahiwi Tomoana is head of our iwi, a funny, innovative statesman with a great presence who is a distant relative and used to work overseas with Pita Sharples. The iwi owns us 100 per cent and we manage the assets for them.

Historically, our biggest assets were deep-water fishing for hoki and orange roughy. We used to lease a boat and the company was very passive with their quota, but we have kicked up the operations. We bought a boat that went out this year from the top of the South Island and have shares in a company, Fiordland Lobster, that exports live crayfish.

It is the biggest company in Australasia by some way with a couple of hundred million bucks' turnover. It is run out of Te Anau and deals in live lobster. They are caught and put in tanks where the water temperature is decreased to put them to sleep, then they are packed in polystyrene bins and sent to China. We hear about processing food, but with crayfish the less you can do the more valuable it is.

We fly them out of Christchurch and Auckland; we bought a huge depot in East Tamaki.

The iwi has been building resources and were in discussions about buying a fishing company in Hawke's Bay for table fish like tarakihi and gurnard, and it bought into a farm four years ago. We have six directors and I am the executive director of our iwi, which extends from Mahia all the way to the bottom of Wairarapa and the top of Wellington. I'm also on the Hawke's Bay Airport board and Hawke's Bay Regional Investment Council, and working on those boards occupies about half my time.

About four years ago Jo and I started a freeze-dried food company called Kiwigarden, with my father-in-law as the main shareholder. It is the largest operation of its kind in the southern hemisphere. While New Zealand is our shop window, it takes only about 5 per cent of our market and the rest is export. We launched a brand of kids' freeze-dried snacks with apples, kiwifruit, banana and other fruit yoghurt drops for kids from nine months to 10 years. It's an overseas idea that we adapted.

Although it lost money for the first few years, we are now selling into China, Singapore, Hong Kong and Malaysia, maybe Australia in a while. Jo runs that business while I am more the sounding board.

Carbon credits is about a three-week job now, Kiwigarden keeps me busy, then working as a director of Fiordland Lobster, the Hawke's Bay Airport work and the regional council, which looks after issues like the port at Napier.

When I left London, I did not envisage this as my life. The rugby was full-on, but I got sick of it, and it became a job and then a slog because as a 30-year-old I had to train all the time doing the same things as a 17-year-old, although we were at very different stages of our careers. I wasn't going to get any faster, but it wasn't till near the end that the coaches tailored my training.

Back home the Maori Agricultural College, which had famous old boys like Louis Paewai and George Nepia, hadn't won a game for three years when they conned me into going along, saying hello and giving them a pep-up. I played a few seasons for them but stopped because I was coaching my kids and the overlap was too much.

The only reason Jo let me play was because the college staff are Mormons and there was no drinking. Playing away was good, because I'd play lock for the second half of a game and then have two beers. If I trained, I couldn't play because I'd be too sore. Playing lock was easy as you just pushed. It was great fun being with a family club and with people enjoying life.

The Randells are Mormons, and have been going back all the way to the 1930s. My grandparents were bishops and on the way to the races or the beach on Sundays, my parents would drop me off at my grandparents to go to church.

Our kids have been involved in the church. I accompanied them on a trip to Utah, which was the most stunning, interesting trip I've ever been on. Our kids were in an academy that Paul Henare started. Every two years the academy has a trip to Utah, while members of the Utah Jazz have been out to Flaxmere on missions. We embraced it and on the first night there we were billeted and had prayers and got involved.

The Mormons have an amazing health benefit system and deliver more than the Red Cross; they are very generous and at the same time teach that God will only help those who help themselves. I haven't signed up, but it was fascinating and we're going back next year.

I've been coaching and I looked after Lanson's rugby team for a couple of years before hc got sick of me and went to high school. Now I'm with Tori's team, and Tenara is playing hockey and basketball. It's a great buzz. I love it and want to help them enjoy it.

We take the kids to school then work school hours, pick them up, give them dinner, take them to sport and then we might go for a walk to discuss things or do some work after dinner. We don't watch a lot of TV, but I manage to see Otago games, the Highlanders, All Blacks tests and the Magpies.

When our kids go to basketball we do a gym session at the same time, or in the morning if they are in the gym we'll go as well, but I don't push too hard. I'm just over my playing weight at 117 kg but I've got heavy bones, and I taste more of the grape than beer. Hawke's Bay is great, and the social and business side of life are both going well.

ERIC RUSH

Eric Rush was better known as the long-time captain and stalwart of hugely successful New Zealand Sevens teams. He featured in nine tests as an All Black over 1992 to 1996, scoring five test tries. He played for the Chiefs in Super Rugby and turned out for Auckland and North Harbour.

Sevens carried me through to 2005 well after my last game for the All Blacks.

It wasn't only Jonah who came along; Jeff Wilson, Christian Cullen and Glen Osborne were always going to play tests ahead of me. They shifted me out to the wing because there were so many great loosies like Michael Jones and Zinny Brooke and then they thought I was too small. The first guy I marked on the wing was Samoa's Lolani Koko who was an absolute monster.

I got 29 games for the All Blacks that I never thought I'd get, including nine tests.

The sevens circuit started in 1996 and New Zealand asked me to help get it up and running and gave me a long contract.

Sevens was a passion of mine and Gordon Tietjens — Titch — was right into it as well. It paid well enough and I'd also got into a bit of property speculation and once I finished playing there was always the speaking circuit.

Initially, I trained as a lawyer and qualified in 1988 before working for six or seven years with Bryan Williams and Kevin McDonald who gave me my first job, which was mostly conveyancing, before rugby went professional.

Everyone thinks we were right in there with the squabbles between NZR and the World Rugby Corporation and others, but we walked into a room in South Africa at the end of the 1995 World Cup and Richie Guy told us rugby was going to be professional the following year. We'd all get $30,000 a year and we were thinking that would be sweet.

We were earning virtually nothing back then — only tour expenses — so $30,000 was a lot of money. We were stoked. It was more than I got as a lawyer, which was a solid job and good training but never really smoked my wheels.

Then WRC said they would pay each of us US$700,000 and we are saying 'Hang on a minute.' Super League was also happening and every back at the World Cup was offered $300,000 to $400,000 to play in that, so Rupert Murdoch was the same guy offering 30K for one competition and $300,000 for the other. We wanted to know his priorities.

I was pretty happy playing amateur rugby where we could play for the right reasons. Guys now get really good money, but they've never known what it's like to play with your mates and trying to crack a rep team. Now they miss selection and are working at who they'll play for overseas. You can't blame them because we would be the same today, that's how it is. I don't begrudge them.

When I started playing rugby for a living, I thought that was the perfect world, doing something I loved and getting good money, but I knew it wasn't going to last so decided that whatever my next job was it had to be something I enjoyed.

You have to work too long not to enjoy it. I kept playing until I was 39 and people asked whether professional rugby changed my life and I said, 'No, but professional rugby changed my wife.' Overnight it changed from 'Hey, you have to knock this rugby on the head and get a job and grow up' to 'You haven't been for a run for two days; get out there and get fit because we have to get a house out of this before you finish.'

The 2002 Commonwealth Games were in Manchester and Titch was getting on my case about not going to the gym. I hated it — gym was the guy on the wing to me. I told him that I'd done well enough without it all my life, so if he didn't think I was good enough then don't pick me.

He used to confide in me all the time but treated me like one of the others building up to that tournament, which was his way of telling me if I didn't scrub up then I'd be axed.

I did the minimum amount of gym work but knew he had to pick me because he rang after the trials to ask me how I went, and I told him I was his best player. 'Stuff it. You were,' he said, and we were back under way again.

After we won the gold, Titch said we know the end is coming but agreed I should make that decision when I knew I wasn't cutting it any more. At that stage, I was still better than the others, but two years later I had three leg injuries in a row and when you are 39 the body is saying 'I can't do it any more.'

We decided that would be it, so I thought about coaching, but playing alright doesn't mean you can coach. I tried to get a sevens job at the nationals and there wasn't one until the

Auckland job came up, which was perfect as they hadn't won the title for about 15 years.

They could all play, but the selections were rough. If the coach was from Ponsonby he picked all those players, as did a coach from Waitemata or Suburbs, while none of the rep players wanted to be involved. They were contracted but didn't bother with sevens, so I sent an e-mail to every club coach in Auckland asking for anyone who thought they were good enough.

We had 80 guys turn up at the first session and I flogged them. You weed them out quickly with fitness and that began with three hours of running, and half of them didn't come back. DJ Forbes was one of those guys in the first year who didn't make my team because he wasn't fit enough, but I gave him a plan and by the next year his whole body shape had changed. He also had a big ticker.

We won the competition four years in a row and I was able to stir up Titch, who never won the nationals, and ask him: 'What was so hard about that?' 'Come and talk to me about hard when you win three Commonwealth Games medals,' he said. He was special because there aren't many coaches who can stay at that level and be successful for such a long time.

I also coached my sons out at East Tamaki where the talent is unbelievable, but that is their biggest enemy because it's too easy, and I tell them they are all big bullies who love bowling little rivals. I warn them that one day that little white fella over there is going to catch you up physically and if he's worked his arse off and you haven't, guess who's going to get in all the teams. That's when it changes and all the McCaws, Carters, Conrad Smiths come through. Maybe that's the problem with the Blues now.

Half our team did not have a phone and it's a real bugger

when it rains because you can only reach half of them. They don't have a watch either, but luckily most of them live within walking distance of the club so we'd have 25 to 30 guys there training every week.

The thing I enjoyed when I was growing up was travelling to Rotorua, Auckland, New Plymouth and Whangarei and I saw all these different places through rugby and thought it was a good deal. Kids now are like I used to be — they think Otara is New Zealand because that's all they have seen.

I get them and their parents together at the start of the year and explain that Auckland is not New Zealand and you can't see the real New Zealand until you get out and see other places. Wenderholm is their idea of up north. I tell them: 'Man, there's another three hours past there,' and they're wide-eyed.

I'd take my team out of Auckland and one year I wanted to take them to Taupo and then snowboarding at Ruapehu.

Before that I got invited by Robin Brooke to speak at a Foodstuffs conference and I took the mickey out of him and spoke about the kids I coached in Otara. The local Foodstuffs guy Vern Heydon, at Pak 'n Save Manukau, who is now retired, and Jason Witehira, who was at Botany New World and now Victoria Park, from the supermarkets either side of the club, said if you need a hand with those kids give us a yell because that's what we do in our community.

Two weeks later we were going to the snow. We had 22 players at East Tamaki and I asked for a few parents to help. Ninety-seven people put their names down for the trip when I had fundraised enough for one bus and to stay in the shearers' quarters at a farm near Taupo.

I had enough money for four days' food for 23 people and one bus. I went to Vern and said, 'You told me to come ask, so here I am.' He rang Jason at New World and between them they paid for both buses and gave us all the food for four days. It was a brilliant gesture.

I was so grateful and told them I couldn't pay them back, but Vern said, 'You're going to pay me back alright. You are going to work in my produce department for nothing for a week.'

'That's easy, no sweat,' I told him. I started at the supermarket at 5 am and finished at 3.30 in the afternoon and all I did was cut cabbages then a pallet of cauliflower and a pallet of lettuce, and then I'd start again. By the end of the week they were letting me split the celery and make up some orders in between sweeping floors and pushing trolleys. They were long days, but it wasn't so bad.

We got to Friday and Vern invited us all to a lunch he put on and then asked us to pay up. They all put $10 on the table and I had no cash on me and told the boss I didn't realise we needed to pay for lunch. He said, 'Nah, nah, nah, all these bastards said you wouldn't be here by Friday.'

After that meeting Vern sat me down and said, 'In this business we don't like guys who are millionaires or think they are clever, we don't want investors; we want people to come into the store and work hard. We gave you all the shitty jobs and you are an All Black from South Auckland where everyone knows you, but none of that worried you.'

He suggested I knuckle down, give it three months and that I'd know if I liked it by then. He said, 'I'll know if you are any good and I'll tell you, so after that time we'll have another talk.' That rang a bell and I worked at Manukau for three months, without pay.

Once that finished, Vern said you can apply to join the group, but Foodstuffs said I needed a job to get some experience, so I went back to Vern and he said, 'Funnily enough, I've got a job coming up.' The Pak 'n Save grocery manager was finishing off his New World training and I moved in to a vacancy as chilled foods manager, as part of the Foodstuffs, Pak 'n Save, New World, Four Square group that's Foodstuffs in New Zealand.

Vern didn't like losing money and told me to learn fast. On my second day, we sold out of chocolate yoghurt and I learned all about milk, butter, yoghurt, bacon, salami, luncheon and all that sort of stuff. After a year, I went back to Foodstuffs, who said I was in their sights but not just yet.

You can join the company as an external like me where you start mid-rung and finance your own way or from the ground up like Vern, whose first job was in Rotorua riding a bicycle delivering groceries, and Jason, who began trimming cabbages at New World in the same city.

My wife Raina was working, and we'd bought and done up a few houses in Otara, so I had a few bob. Lots of external guys have a nest egg and can afford it, but internals learn everything about the business from the bottom up.

I was based for three years at Manukau Pak 'n Save then a year at New World Botany doing every single job until, in 2010, after a whole lot of interviews, I became an approved owner-operator at Browns Bay New World. That was almost as good as making the All Blacks because I'd worked so hard for it. It was the same process, going through club rugby to your province then the professional ranks if you are good enough — you have to go through all the steps.

I sold my houses to get into Browns Bay New World, which was a small and old supermarket and hard work but rewarding. They were 18-hour days, which is no snack, and in the first two years I had about two weeks off and some of that was for my mum's funeral. I had 55 staff and was responsible for all of them. Whenever any of them moaned about their hours, I asked them if they wanted to swap jobs because I knew the answer. I had three years there before moving in 2013 to Kaikohe when the company asked if I'd like to move because I was from up that way.

I'd always been keen to go home, but with Mum and Dad gone I wasn't in quite such a hurry and we'd lived in Auckland for 30 years. However, from a commercial point of view it was better if I got stuck into it.

It was a nice shop in a tough town and very busy. The bad guys, the opposition Countdown, are in town too, but we kept each other honest, then last August I moved to run the Regent New World with a staff of close to 200 in Whangarei, where there is another New World, three Countdowns and a Pak 'n Save.

Some days you deal with a lady whose cat is the most important thing in her life, then there might be some Black Power guys giving us grief about the price of grog, or staff problems, but I like how there are separate businesses under the same roof; the butchery is separate from the chilled foods and groceries, and you have to get the team pulling in the same direction.

From Taupo north there are 48 New Worlds and we have a strong market share in New Zealand. I can ring any branch if I've got an issue, as it is a big family, all with similar issues.

When I came down to school in Auckland I met my wife Raina who became a rugby widow and was becoming a supermarket widow, so I gave her a job in the office. We have five kids, my daughter Natalie is 25, lives on the Gold Coast and has a son and twin boys who are 23 — Blair plays rugby in Newcastle but has done his knee, and Martyn, who is into jiu-jitsu.

I coach my two younger boys: Brady, who is at Westlake because of his mates, and Rob, who is on a scholarship at Saint Kentigern. I never pushed the two older boys because I was playing, but they all work hard at their games and enjoy it.

Watching rugby from the sidelines occupies a fair chunk of my time and I take in games on television.

One day I was speaking to Jason Witehira about my supermarket work and said, 'I wish I'd done this a bit earlier,' and he said, 'I wish I'd been an All Black.'

JOHN TIMU

John Timu debuted for the All Blacks in 1989 and played mostly at fullback until 1994, appearing in 50 tests and scoring seven test tries. He represented Otago at provincial level. He switched to rugby league and played for the Canterbury Bulldogs and London Broncos.

The silly thing is I'm still running around on the football field. Not very often, but I get out with a Golden Oldies team called the Wrinkly Rams here in the Upper Clutha and we play about twice a year. It wasn't too good a few years ago when I snapped my Achilles tendon and my wife Kas said, 'That's it, you're retired.' But I got back on the field again. I enjoy getting amongst it and there are plenty of cobwebs to blow out.

I'm a project manager for Breen Construction who are an Alexandra-based company and have been around for about 80 years in Central and North Otago with branches in Wanaka, Cromwell, Oamaru and Dunedin.

I'm getting a bit long in the tooth and thought I'd better

future-proof myself a bit, so I've been off the tools and working for myself for about two and a half years and have gone more into project management. It's a nice fit; I'm still out and about with the boys on site and dealing with the foremen or leading hands on projects. The role is a lot more flexible and with the cold winters down here I can mix it up a bit by going to the sites or sitting in the office in front of the heat pump.

After switching from rugby in 1994, I had three years of rugby league with the Bulldogs in Sydney then another three with the Broncos in London. I then needed to get my teeth into something rather than running around on the footy field, so we went back to Sydney where I did an adult building apprenticeship.

That took four years before we came back to New Zealand with our four children. Three were born in Australia and one in London, so we've got one that whinges all the time and three that think they know it all. It peed me off when my oldest sings the Aussie national anthem at Wallaby games, so we had to get the kids back home growing up as Kiwis. We always thought we'd be back by the time the eldest, Josh, was ready to start school, but he was seven and our youngest just six months.

We go boy, girl, girl, boy and next year they'll all be in Dunedin. Josh is studying accounting and finance, Meg is last year at St Hilda's, Annie is there too, and Jack is in Year 8 and next year will go to John McGlashan College.

Wanaka is a great place and we love it here. Mount Aspiring College is brilliant, but my wife and I both went to boarding school and we like the independence it teaches kids, so they were all going away somewhere. It's going to be interesting with just the pair of us here and it's always hard when any of the kids leave home. We'll still see them a lot because we spent a lot of time in Dunedin and we'll spend even more time down there I guess. It will be great being on the coast and we'll make the most of it because we are landlocked up here.

We're like a lot of ex-All Blacks my age, chasing kids around and watching them on sports fields all over the place. It's interesting who you run into on the side of the netball court, rugby field, at rowing or at multi-sports events.

When I finished with league I always wanted to get into construction because I've always been reasonably handy. When I left New Zealand in 1994 and went to the Bulldogs we bought a house over there that you'd call a doer-upper. I played alongside lots of blokes who went through the trades and thought it would suit me after I stopped chasing a footy ball.

It was a commitment being an adult apprentice but a stepping-stone position that had to be taken. I enjoyed it and miss being on the tools now. There are actually plenty of jobs I'm supposed to do at home, but they are on the back burner. Kas had the idea that I should get off the tools and work as a project manager and initially I was sceptical, but it was a good move and it has future-proofed me a bit as well. I'm starting to feel the cold more on site and have to admit to Kas that she was right, as she is most of the time.

She works for a firm in town doing administration and payroll and enjoys it. From the time we met when we were students, Kas has worked all the way through apart from having four children, which is a job in itself. I tried to help, but I think I'm a bit like the fifth child.

We thought we might come home for good after my last Super League season in the UK, so we bought a campervan and tiki-toured around the North Island, catching up with friends and family we hadn't seen for ages and spending some time at the Mount to see if it ticked the boxes. We'd both worked there during varsity holidays and enjoyed it, but it didn't click for us as a family. We thought that rather than make a rash decision, we still had a house in Sydney that was only across the Ditch, so it was easy to come back and forth, although it also meant a four-year stint because of this apprenticeship.

We loved our time there living at Dolans Bay on the Port Hacking River near Cronulla where the boat ramp was close, the surf was nearby, and we had the national park just below us, but it just wasn't home. I studied in town at Randwick and worked for my trade and builder's licences at the same time so that I could operate a business rather than restricting myself to being an employee. It gave me a lot more knowledge about all the processes and I wanted those extra strings to my bow because I was going to be working for myself back here and wanted to give myself every bit of assistance.

I played rugby through the amateur era, but those years in the league pro ranks gave us a good head start for getting into a career outside footy. If I'd stayed in union, who knows what would have happened?

As a teenager I was peppered with league offers, but there were things I wanted to do in rugby and I had aspirations of becoming an All Black and doing well. I think I always knew I was going to switch and I don't know if there is ever a good time. I wanted to go when I could give it a decent crack and watched Inga Tuigamala, Matthew Ridge and Craig Innes head to league, and the benefit for them was they went at an age when they were still young and their bodies were strong.

I didn't want to go at the end of my career. I was 25 when I switched and thought I had a few good years left. It was a big decision to turn your back on the All Blacks jersey, especially leading into a World Cup, and there was a lot of soul-searching about that and I still vaguely remember watching the ABs in the 1995 final as a lot of Kiwis would.

It was a significant occasion where you remember where you were at the time and it felt like a bit of a disaster weekend. I watched the World Cup final early in the morning and we all know the result. Earlier that day, the Bulldogs had played Newcastle and we got a record thumping and I got injured in the match too, so the whole day felt like a write-off.

We don't realise how spoiled we are as rugby fans to see how well the All Blacks are playing and how dominant the team has been through Richie's era and today. It is phenomenal. I'm not great with statistics, but I've got an idea when I played it was always 50–50 whether we would beat Australia. A lot of the time they had the wood on us, and we never won anything like the number of games the team does now.

The All Blacks have a great culture, which is brilliant. I think New Zealand took a while to embrace professionalism, but once we ironed out a few things, we became successful. We use what we have got and nine times out of 10 we come up with the goods. Remember we don't have the same kind of financial backing of others because of our small population — just look at the America's Cup.

I've probably been yachting four times in my life and I capsized once, but the 2017 America's Cup had the whole country enthralled. Likewise, the All Blacks in the 2015 RWC were seamless; they went about their job, they got on with it. It was like I was watching that 2015 RWC again with the yachting — they knew how they were going about things and for them to do that after the previous campaign was amazing.

Everyone loves the sort of rugby challenge the Lions came

up with on their tour and a lot of Kiwis would like the Wallabies to be more competitive than they have been recently — but not too good! No one likes a mismatch and that filters down the grades and even into junior boys' rugby. This year in Central we have eight junior teams and there is an even standard right through the competition and that's great; working to get a result feels even more special.

When we came home from Sydney for good, we had four kids, so we were definitely going to be near some grandparents. We have enjoyed bringing up the kids and having them as part of our lives and we have worked hard to achieve that and be independent, but there were times when babysitters were important.

Hawke's Bay was an option, but in the interim we had bought a holiday home in Wanaka and my in-laws had retired and built here, and as scarfies we'd spend a lot of time around here skiing.

We also had a couple of acres south of Dunedin at Blackhead, which is a surf spot, and the idea was we could stay at Wanaka for a while and I could build the family home at Blackhead. However, the plan got flipped on its head, which might have been Kas's masterplan, as we sold our holiday home and put our roots down at Wanaka. The kids had become ingrained in school here and it is a good place to live. While I was sulking a bit because it was so far from the coast, I had to make the most of it.

During holidays we'll get down to places like Curio Bay in Southland where we can get amongst it with some fishing, diving and surfing. There's no cellphone coverage so it's just talking and enjoying ourselves even if the weather is rubbish. That's good Kiwi living, and you have to make the most of it wherever you are.

In three years in London we didn't come home because we always knew that was on the cards for later, but our parents came to visit and we travelled to a lot of places throughout Europe. It doesn't work out that way for everyone. I've got quite a few mates who married foreign girls and that makes it difficult because someone has to make a sacrifice when deciding where to live, but I married a Southland girl, which makes it easier.

With my passion for the outdoors, I hunt with the boys, we go diving, we have a boat — although the kaimoana is a bit short in the lake — we go water-skiing, skiing and snowboarding.

Wanaka is not the small village it once was, but we enjoy the feel of the place. We live out of town on some acres because when all six of us are here we like making a bit of noise and there is plenty of space for people to come and stay — it's always great to have friends and relatives under the same roof. We've got about 20 lambs we fatten and send away to the works each year and seem to be breeding lots of rabbits, but I'm no farmer and don't have green fingers, although I'm good at cutting down old pines for firewood.

We're going to be chasing our kids for a while longer yet. I coached Jack at rugby and cricket, but he will be in town next year and needs another coach rather than his old man. I also help out with the local premier rugby side, but that's not a big commitment.

Breen Construction are good employers and my role is flexible. If I'm really busy I can be mobile with my laptop, dealing with architects and buyers. I've been looking after a build in Twizel so have to go there to talk to the foreman and in winter it can get a bit hairy travelling through the Lindis Pass. But I have a four-wheel drive and put the chains on. Living in Wanaka you always have to travel for sport, and generally people are pretty good driving in the winter conditions.

Sometimes I might have to look after something in Queenstown, but 90 per cent of my work is in Wanaka. It's a big company with about 180 employees and we do everything from home maintenance and fitting a door lock to building bridges, designer construction and commercial projects. I'm still learning and it's different from doing the residential builds I was involved in for about a decade.

Building is always about problem-solving, which is good because there are things like digging footings or painting that I'm not too keen on and I wouldn't want to be in the industry if I was only involved with frames or trusses. Most people would find it hard to get motivated if they were doing the same thing day after day, but I am doing the whole kit and caboodle in this job.

JEFF WILSON

In an illustrious All Blacks career spanning 1993–99 and 2001, 'Goldie' totalled 234 points in 60 tests, including three tries on debut. He played for the Highlanders in Super Rugby and for Southland and Otago provincial teams. He also represented New Zealand in cricket.

G ive me a choice between coaching the All Blacks or getting in the sulky and driving the Interdominion pacing favourite, I think I'd take the reins. I'm not likely to do either, but it would be a massive thrill.

Since I stopped playing, I've stayed close to the action working for Sky and was so proud interviewing the All Blacks after they won the World Cup again in 2015 and telling people how good they were.

In my job, I wondered if it could get any better than that test at Twickenham. I'm not sure it can, but you always strive for the next thing, and if somehow I ended up on the favourite — hopefully trained by Mark Purdon — that would be on another level again.

An appetite for experiencing different ideas has pushed me in many directions. I'm not sure I like routine or staying with the same old, same old for too long and that was behind my decision to give cricket another crack once my time with the All Blacks was up.

It's ticked over 15 years since my rugby days with my last All Blacks season in 2001, then a year with the Highlanders before I redirected my sporting concentration to cricket.

I started by moving from a standard house in Dunedin to Christchurch and buying 120 acres of bare land outside Burnham. That was a serious change of scenery, but it was close to Lincoln where I needed to prepare for what I hoped would be a return to first-class cricket.

My uncle was a former Southland farmer who lived five kilometres away and Adine, who worked in the city as a lawyer, has a farming background too, but I was a rural rookie.

Trying to manage our rural property and playing first-class cricket in the summer were real learning experiences, while I also wanted to increase my knowledge of the horse-racing industry and experience the training side of things. That was my work for the next few years as Adine commuted to Invercargill to play netball and I drove to Dunedin to play my cricket.

New Zealand Cricket was very supportive, allowing me to train at the facilities in Lincoln with their coaches as well as work with Glenn Turner in Dunedin.

My sporting focus altered course rather than stopped. After an early taste of cricket then a good spell with the All Blacks, I wanted to see how far I could go in cricket again. It was another chapter in carving out a life after rugby, although I did get a taste for coaching rugby at Murray Mexted's academy in Palmerston North.

Our schedules were hectic, but we didn't have any kids and it was possible to mix up a lot of things.

I knew how to play cricket, but physically I was nowhere near becoming a bowler again because my body had changed shape after nine years playing rugby, I'd been through a couple of ankle operations and my body balance was unsuited to cricket.

All the things that had been instinctive were not quite happening. My brain was telling me one thing and my body was telling me another, and that was frustrating. I'd have liked to play longer, but in the end, it wasn't meant to be.

My idea was to be a bowler. That was the thing I loved to do, and I believe that was the strongest part of my game, but as much as I tried my body did not allow me to do it. I was very determined, but my game never quite got back to where I hoped.

My weight dropped a bit and I finished at 97 kg, but the way those muscles moved was very different from a decade earlier. I went from a lot of natural movement to powerful movement and that did not suit fast bowling. All the bowlers you see now are tall and lean and very flexible; it's a different game. The frustrations came because I was inconsistent in how I felt and performed, and that was hard when you were fighting against your body.

My life balance came with the support from Adine and getting back to the farm and trying to educate myself about that lifestyle, something I knew little about other than being shipped out to my uncle's farm in Invercargill in the school holidays, tackling ewes and lambing and getting up first thing in the morning.

Our land in Christchurch was a grazing farm and in summer we moved irrigation systems, fertilised the paddocks, talked to contractors and all those details and then in winter we would feed dairy cows for about 10 to 12 weeks, which worked for me because it was my downtime.

I was an average farmer. My hands are for sport, not fixing equipment, fencing or mending troughs. I am not good with machinery or engines and I vividly remember the first day we got a John Deere tractor. I managed to smash the door off it then backed the irrigator into a fence — those sorts of things seemed to follow me around the farm.

Some stock are not the most intelligent beasts and while you might fix things one day, or try to, they break it the next. You'd set the electric fence and find an animal on the wrong side of it the next morning. Fortunately, Adine held it together and the neighbouring farmers were very understanding and helpful.

Being on the farm was different, a lifestyle choice, a great experience and a really good look at being self-sufficient — and we loved it. It built up my love of harness racing and we bought another 30 acres nearby to look after our horses.

That passion started with visits to Ascot Park in Invercargill. I don't breed horses any more or drive them, but I'm hugely interested and fascinated by the industry and go to Cup week in Christchurch whenever I can.

There is no better feeling than conditioning your horse with the thrill of sorting out the tactics and getting a win, whether it is a maiden or group one race, and being on course with your mates having a few beers.

Breeding was an interest and we had one good one, but she went mad. It is an industry that is battling for its place now and sometimes the dubious sides of it, like gambling, are highlighted, but the number of people it supports and entertains as an industry outweighs the cons.

I'll have a punt, but only an interest bet, and certainly don't bet enough to lose any sleep over it.

As my return to cricket began to peter out, I got into more work at the International Rugby Academy of New Zealand (IRANZ), which is such an undervalued asset in this country. This fired my interest about getting into coaching, so I rang Tony Gilbert, who was working with Otago Rugby, and he encouraged me to pursue that course.

I ended up working on the administration side for the province, while my uncle looked after the farm and leased it for grazing horses.

In hindsight, I was probably not ready for that job, and 15 months there convinced me I was not ready to be in the office. They were great people to work with, but it was eye-opening to experience all the politics that went on behind the scenes, which you are not really privy to or interested in when you are playing.

Getting players to move to Dunedin was a struggle. The pattern of university students combining study and rugby had faded and there were battles about whether Otago or the Highlanders should pay and recruit players. A lot of it was out of our hands.

I actually wanted to be outside and thought I was better suited to working with the players.

Otago had their coaches and I was working at IRANZ where the time with coaches and players was absorbing and really nourishing and a great boost to me in my coaching ideas. I met Craig Dowd, who was at North Harbour after coming back from playing in England, and we got together in 2009 to coach the union.

Neither of us had played for Harbour, so that was an issue,

and on the home front Adine had just had our son Harper and was still in Invercargill.

Moving was the first step but the best decision we have made. The 150-acre farm was sold while Adine's talents found us a great place to live in Auckland. We love living here, as there are so many fantastic opportunities and things to do in this city and our boys, Harper and Lincoln have settled in really well. It is warmer and anyone who says otherwise is lying. The people are great and there are so many choices.

Coaching Harbour was tough, and I did not fully understand the scene until I was immersed in it. There were only a few schools who played rugby, limited feeder systems into clubs and so many other attractions for kids. Rangitoto College, for example, is a huge school but doesn't really have a rugby system so there are those challenges on the Shore which Auckland and its established systems do not have.

We knew what we were operating with compared to other teams and that's the way it was. It was competing for players and talent . . . and thinking about what to do in the future. After Craig moved on, Liam Barry came in as head coach at North Harbour and we formed a coaching team. Although we had limited success on the field, I enjoyed the environment and we became good mates along the way.

In my last year at Harbour, I got an opportunity to do some work at the Blues with Pat Lam in the final challenging year of his coaching tenure. We lost Jerome Kaino and Isaia Toeava to injury at the start of the season then struggled. I was promoted to work on the defence for the last few games, but the end was coming.

John Kirwan took over as coach and I got to know him really well. We used to be competitors and I took his jersey and he took my coaching role. His attitude and the way he lives his life is superb and the people he helps consistently through his work with depression is immense.

Around that time, I started doing a little commentary work for Sky while I was doing my provincial rugby coaching. It was intense. Coaching a provincial side is brutal because you have about three weeks' lead-in with your Super Rugby players to establish a culture, get your game plans together then be competitive and somehow develop the players as you go through.

You sit there and if you've got a big gap in your work commitments you think about what you might do in the future. Luckily, I had done a little commentary with Keith Quinn at the RWC when they rang and asked me to go and assist at a few games in Australia. He was very helpful with how to deliver my comments and cope with the processes in television.

I didn't think too much about it. It was a one-off, but live television was unnerving. I was there to do comments, but every now and then I'd be asked to do a cross and I had no training for that, so it was nerve-racking.

When you leave the playing arena you think those nerves will go, but television brought them all back with the whole dynamic of starting at the bottom and trying to learn a new craft while someone is talking in your ear and you are supposed to be listening to others.

Some of the early stuff I did was horrific, but it was on-the-job training, and once you get over yourself and don't take yourself so seriously you have to think about what people want to hear.

I moved onto some panels for Sky without doing any commentary, just being the guy on the end of questions. I'm not a newsreader; I am a passionate rugby fan who is trying to help people understand the game. As long as I keep bringing myself back to that, I tend to enjoy it more and deliver in better ways.

The keys are much the same as playing sport — preparation and research.

I needed a break from coaching, but it was a wrench leaving Liam Barry because he is a terrific man and it is good to see him working in the sevens environment in Tauranga. He is a fantastic coach, but circumstances did not work out for us and JK was coming into the Blues with his own crew that he wanted to work with.

I got a chance to learn another craft and different skills working at LiveSport radio with Ian Smith and Nathan Rarere, people who love their sport — Nathan with his wide knowledge and passion for a multitude of sports and Smithy who is across our two main sports in a big way and is one of our best broadcasters.

Radio interviews were great. I'd been there two weeks when I was told to go and interview Greg Norman. Are you kidding me? It was a fantastic chance, but I was a rookie sent to talk to one of the greats of golf who also had a huge business empire. I started off with something innocuous and he gave me four minutes' worth without saying much.

I had 64,000 questions because I was massively overprepared when the trick is to do your preparation, listen to the conversation and use your research to extract interesting answers. My interview was okay, just average, but what a start.

For about 15 months radio was great, but my kids were getting older and demanding more of my time and after the early starts I was running out of juice late in the day. Work began to impinge on the rest of my life and interfere with that enjoyment.

People ask me how busy I am, and I tell them I spend a lot of time preparing for a minimal outcome, but at the start I didn't know anything about that because I hadn't been to broadcasting school or journalism courses to find out how it all worked.

You often find yourself rephrasing a question because you are looking to flesh out an answer or get some more information about an issue. Radio was good, but Sky wanted more from me and watching Smithy try to juggle both helped me make choices. Radio had to be the sacrifice because Sky was a better family fit.

I'm also wary about getting overexposed after hearing the same stuff from the same people over and over. Fresh is best, rather than being a repetitive soundbite.

Now I'm a host and I have to guard against it just being a job; it has to be a passion. I believe in the integrity of performance and I've met some great people and others who perhaps should look at why they are there.

Like so many professions, it comes down to time in the saddle. Doing more and more and getting more comfortable, making sure you are organised — it's no different from being an athlete. You just have to prepare your brain differently. My enjoyment and preparation has changed and now I am at the point where I am enjoying it. We're trying to produce something a little different as the media world evolves.

I prefer commentary because I love the game, but there is not much between the work and I understand the roles you have to play. I love being sideline or commenting, fronting test matches is great and hosting *The Breakdown* programme is a different dynamic to drive, because the guests' guns are loaded with different perspectives and banter. We try to be thorough and help people understand what the game is all about.

The feedback you get shows you how much television is a part of people's lives and how much rugby is a centrepiece of conversation and discussion in New Zealand.

In a decade's time I'm not sure what I'll be doing because I've never been one to look into the future too much. I'll work for Sky for the next couple of years and see what happens then. I don't like overcommitting myself because my standards are high, and I'm someone with itchy feet who never believes in wasting time and opportunities.

AFTERWORD — By Dr John Mayhew

I am delighted to be able to contribute this final chapter to Wynne's book. In many ways our 'sporting' careers have paralleled each other. We have both observed the national game from close proximity as it transitioned from the amateur era — pre-1996 — through to the modern game and the advent of full-blown professionalism. And while we obviously view the game from different perspectives, both of us have, you might say, been on 'rugby watch' for close to 40 years.

In this time, Wynne has developed a reputation as one of the most incisive rugby writers in the country, while my career as a sports doctor has seen me attached to a number of prominent New Zealand teams, including the All Blacks and the Warriors.

As you will have already read, Wynne has focused on players whose careers straddled both the amateur and professional eras. For the most part, these players have gone on to enjoy successful careers post-rugby, but I would like to offer some views on the modern-day professional.

First, I think it was far easier for players to transition out of the amateur era and into the professional ranks back in the 90s. Many of the players from that latter era of amateur rugby already had other professions or were working towards building one.

Nowadays, though, things are vastly different. And, despite public perception, it's not that easy to learn other skills while you're a full-time rugby player. The guys at the elite level in both rugby and rugby league basically work 8 am to 5 pm jobs. They train hard, they play hard and they fulfil a lot of community and commercial commitments.

One of my biggest concerns is around what happens to these professional players after their careers are over. All the indices point to the fact they do very badly. We should be taking notice of what's happened overseas. Just look at English football where retired players have struggled financially, emotionally and psychologically. The levels of bankruptcy, broken marriages and drug dependency are frightening.

I talk to a lot of players after their careers are over, after the adulation has died away. Many of them struggle with this transition phase — suddenly they have to get up at six o'clock each day and go to a regular job, doing mundane things that most other people have done for years. Suddenly they have become Joe Ordinary.

My personal interest in this area has been driven to a certain extent by the fact my wife and I have three sons who have played professional rugby. Believe me, it's not that easy telling burly rugby players what to do with their lives. Nevertheless, we have always highlighted concerns about their careers post-rugby and encouraged their studies. They get it. They understand. One of the boys has a university degree and the other two are working towards theirs. All three went through rugby academy programmes and part of the deal was tertiary training.

While the academies — both rugby and league — serve a valuable purpose, there's still work to be done on some of the programmes. There are also questions around whether we're getting players into professional sport too early when, really, they've got no life skills.

Afterword — By Dr John Mayhew

It is all very well for these players to get picked up by the big schools and then get fast-tracked into sports academies. But is that really the best outcome? Is it not better for these guys to have a broader school education?

As well, we've got to educate the players' families — make everyone aware that professional sport is a tough career choice and most players simply won't make it. They may well have been brilliant schoolboys but there is a strong chance they won't survive in the professional ranks.

As for putting players into academies while they're still at school. Well, I question that. At the end of the day, you've got to remember that many players who make, say, a Blues or Warriors academy won't become full-time professional footballers at all. And then there are players who might end up making it to the elite tier but may only last 20 or 30 games — just a couple of seasons. There's a danger we're actually jeopardising those young men's long-term futures. Plan A for a player is generally to make it to the top of the tree, but having a Plan B is an absolute must.

That's often when a player agent comes into play. Good agents are worth their weight in gold. We are fortunate in New Zealand that, by and large, we are well served in this area. There are, though, a few agents who think their job is over as soon as their player signs a contract. They grab their percentage and then lose interest.

Instead, player agents should be encouraging their players to invest wisely. Remember, professional sport is an unusual sphere of endeavour. Most athletes' career earnings will peak while they're in their twenties and early thirties. By the time they reach 33 or so and their careers are over, their income may have contracted by as much as 80 per cent. It's just another reason to keep hammering home the value of ongoing education.

One of my real concerns is for the financial well-being of the vast numbers of Polynesian players involved in contact sports in New Zealand. It's obviously a sensitive area, but many provide financial support for their extended families. A lot of the money they earn during their careers won't end up in their own pockets and they can often finish their careers without much at all. To me, they are the most vulnerable players. What happens to them once their careers come to an end? No job training or tertiary education to fall back on and, sadly, not a lot of money . . .

In rugby, I would advocate for some sort of compulsory superannuation scheme — call it Rugby Saver — where players are obligated to put away a certain percentage of their earnings. In turn, it would be gratifying to see the employers meet these player contributions dollar for dollar. I know it's a vexed question and raises all sorts of issues but, to my mind, it would be an important way of protecting the vulnerable young players and ensuring there was something tangible there at the end of the day.

Fortunately, both the New Zealand Rugby Players' Association and the Rugby League Players' Association are now putting schemes in place whereby players post-career can get trained.

Players' physical well-being, both during and after their careers, is another hotly debated issue these days. Medical science can deal with most of the common problems — battered knees, shoulders and the like — but it is, of course, the head injuries that are causing most concern.

It has become a very emotive subject and, to a certain extent, slightly overcooked. There is obviously a clear connection between repeated head injuries and medical issues later in life. But studies have shown that it might not be as linear as some people think.

Recent investigations have attempted to link a number of cases of dementia straight back to concussive injuries sustained in contact sport. While some of this might well be true, the evidence is nowhere near conclusive. In fact, in many cases there were other underlying medical conditions that contributed to the dementia.

There is still no direct correlation between concussions and dementia in later life. In fact, research in the United States has shown that there is evidence that the incidences of CTE (chronic traumatic encephalopathy) amongst the general population is, percentage-wise, the same as amongst contact sports athletes. In saying that, it's still quite hard to quantify because we don't tend to do the sorts of autopsies on the general population that are performed on contact sport athletes.

Having said all this, I am not in any way suggesting that we shouldn't do everything possible to ensure contact sports are safe. Far from it. In fact, today we are seeing vast improvements in rugby and league in the way we are dealing with head injuries both on and off the field.

Both codes now have video available on the sideline to review incidents, in particular, head clashes. We have certain protocols in place for in-game head assessments and the ability to have players withdrawn from a match if we believe there is a further risk to that player. Psychometric testing, which, amongst other things, includes numerical and verbal reasoning, is our barometer. It's obviously not perfect, but it's what we have at the moment. If there was some other test which was, perhaps, more objective, that would be great. We're looking all the time.

As a side note, I am concerned about former players compromising their neurological health through involvement in poorly monitored boxing fights — I am aware of one ex-player whose health was severely compromised by brain injury following an amateur charity fight.

Quite rightly, there is a huge amount of discussion surrounding player welfare in professional sport in this country. By and large, I think rugby is trying its very best. There are a huge number of resources available to these young men. In the end they just have to be steered in the right direction and given good, solid advice. They need reminding that, despite what they might think, they're not bulletproof. Parents and agents should always be pushing for that elusive Plan B.

Education is the number one priority. Sport can be cruel, and dreams may not last.